ISSUE 25, OCTOBER 2025

AUSTRALIAN FOREIGN AFFAIRS

Contributors

Gareth Evans was Australia's Foreign Minister from 1988 to 1996 and president of the International Crisis Group from 2000 to 2009.

Stephan Frühling is a professor at the Strategic and Defence Studies Centre at the Australian National University.

Mark Harrison is a senior lecturer in Chinese Studies at the University of Tasmania.

Gordon Noble is a research director with the Institute for Sustainable Futures at the University of Technology Sydney.

Andrew O'Neil is a professor in the Faculty of Law and Business at Australian Catholic University.

Jennifer Parker is an expert associate at the National Security College, ANU, an adjunct fellow at UNSW and a fellow at the Council on Geostrategy.

Rajeswari (Raji) Pillai Rajagopalan is a resident senior fellow with the Australian Strategic Policy Institute, Canberra.

Brendan Taylor is Professor of Strategic Studies at the Australian National University.

Nick Wood is the director of the consultancy Climate Policy Research.

Australian Foreign Affairs is published three times a year by Australian Foreign Affairs Pty Ltd. Publisher: Morry Schwartz. Editor-in-chief: Erik Jensen. ISBN 978-1-76064-6004 ISSN 2208-5912 Subscriptions: 1-year print and digital subscription (3 issues): $79.00 within Australia incl. GST. 1-year digital-only auto-renew: $49.00. Payment may be made by MasterCard, Visa or Amex, or by cheque made out to Schwartz Books Pty Ltd. Payment includes postage and handling. Subscribe online at www.australianforeignaffairs.com, email subscribe@australianforeignaffairs.com or phone 1800 077 514 / 61 3 9486 0288. Correspondence should be addressed to: The Editor, Australian Foreign Affairs, 22–24 Northumberland Street, Collingwood, VIC, 3066 Australia Phone: 61 3 9486 0288 / Fax: 61 3 9486 0244 Email: enquiries@australianforeignaffairs.com. Editor: Jonathan Pearlman. Deputy Editor: Julian Welch. Associate Editor: Chris Feik. Design: Peter Long. Production Coordination: Marilyn de Castro. Typesetting: Tristan Main. Cover image: Public domain. Printed in Australia by McPherson's Printing Group.

Editor's Note

THE BOMB

At the southern tip of Jervis Bay, New South Wales, is a remote forest that – until John Gorton was ousted as prime minister by his Liberal Party colleagues in March 1971 – was due to house a 500-megawatt nuclear reactor that could have enabled the development of home-grown nuclear weapons.

Gorton, reflecting decades later on the plans for the reactor, recalled: "We were interested in this thing because it could provide electricity to everybody and it could, if you decided later on, make an atomic bomb."

Instead, Gorton tentatively signed the Treaty on the Non-Proliferation of Nuclear Weapons, and Gough Whitlam, weeks after Labor's election victory, eagerly ratified it in January 1973. The Jervis Bay plans were shelved and Australia became one of the world's most active backers of arms controls.

It is worth recalling the two global developments that prompted Gorton to consider a push for the bomb. In October 1964, China had detonated its first nuclear device. An official statement said the weapons were for "protecting the Chinese people from the danger of the

United States launching a nuclear war". Then, in the late 1960s, the United States moved to reduce its involvement in the Vietnam War, raising concerns in Canberra that its closest security ally was retreating from Asia and entering a period of isolationism. Today, similar concerns – about China's growing strength and the United States' commitment to Asia – are again fuelling regional anxieties.

But much has changed since the 1960s. China boomed and became Australia's largest trading partner. The United States re-elected a president who openly questions the benefit of providing military support to partners in need. And North Korea developed nuclear weapons, leaving South Korea and Japan existentially reliant on Washington's commitments to defend them.

This changing equation is prompting countries across Asia to reassess their security options.

In Japan, former deputy defence minister Rui Matsukawa told Reuters in August that concerns about the United States' reliability – especially since Donald Trump's re-election – were prompting Japan to reconsider its defence policy. "Plan B is maybe go independent, and then go nukes," she said.

In South Korea, a strong majority of the population favours developing nuclear weapons. There have been growing calls in Washington to remove obstacles to Seoul going nuclear, including from Elbridge Colby, Trump's under secretary for defense policy. He told South Korea's Yonhap News Agency in 2024 that Seoul would "have to take primary, essentially overwhelming, responsibility for its own self-defence …

because we don't have a military that can fight North Korea and then be ready to fight China".

Today, Australia needs to prepare not only for an increasingly insecure Asia but also for the risk that this insecurity could cause nuclear weapons to spread across the region. Australia must consider how to respond to near-allies such as Japan going nuclear, whether China's nuclear outlook is changing as its ambitions grow, and how it might renew its diplomatic push for arms control in an age of proliferation and as memories of the horrors of Hiroshima and Nagasaki fade.

Australia may also find itself pondering, for the first time in more than fifty years, whether otherwise unthinkable options should be part of its own plan B.

Jonathan Pearlman

BOILING POINT

Preparing for the new nuclear age

Brendan Taylor

Since the dawn of the nuclear age, Australians have looked nervously north. During the Cold War, it was the Soviet Union that cast the longest shadow. Our alliance with the United States and the presence of joint intelligence facilities on Australian soil made us a potential target in any superpower conflict. In the decades that followed, our anxieties shifted to rogue states such as North Korea and Iran, to nuclear terrorism and, most recently, to China's rapidly growing arsenal. The logic has always been simple: nuclear weapons were dangerous because they were in the hands of those who might one day use them against us. That logic has shaped Australian strategy for generations. But what if it no longer holds? What if the next countries to acquire the world's most destructive weapons aren't our enemies but our friends?

This is the unsettling possibility that now confronts Australia. We are entering a new nuclear age, one that looks very different from the Cold War. Power is shifting, alliances are under strain and some of our closest partners are beginning to question whether they can still shelter under America's nuclear umbrella. In Seoul, in Tokyo and perhaps one day in Jakarta, the idea of building independent nuclear forces is no longer unthinkable. These are not hostile states bent on aggression. They are democratic partners with whom we share deep economic and security ties. But if they go nuclear, it will challenge longstanding assumptions, unsettle our alliances and force Australia to confront choices we've long preferred to avoid.

After fading from view in the decades following the Cold War, nuclear weapons are back at the centre of international security. Vladimir Putin's nuclear threats during the war in Ukraine have reminded the world – in the starkest possible terms – of the devastating power these weapons still hold.

Yet the new nuclear age is different. It is not centred in Europe or defined by a single bipolar rivalry. It is more complex, more crowded and much closer to home. Asia is emerging as the new epicentre of nuclear risk – a region where nuclear-armed powers are multiplying, where doctrines diverge and escalation risks are growing. Unlike during the Cold War, the dividing lines are no longer clear. Friends may become nuclear-armed. Alliances may fray or falter under the pressure. And the region could find itself edging towards a new Asian balance of terror far more complex and unstable than the Cold War ever was.

Australia has barely begun to think about what this means. For decades, we've worried about nuclear weapons only when they were in the hands of our enemies, trusting that the US alliance would keep us safe. That assumption no longer holds. In a more contested and unpredictable region, we need to rethink how we live with nuclear weapons. That means understanding not just the capabilities of our adversaries but also the motivations of our closest partners. And it means asking: what should Australia do if the next Asian nuclear domino to fall is one we consider a friend?

South Korea: Most likely

Among Australia's friends, South Korea is the one most seriously weighing the nuclear option. In an April 2025 poll by the Asan Institute for Policy Studies, a record 76 per cent of South Koreans supported the development of a nuclear arsenal. That sentiment reflects a harsh reality. North Korea's atomic arsenal has grown markedly in recent years, both in size and diversity. The Stockholm International Peace Research Institute estimates that it possesses enough fissile material to produce up to ninety nuclear warheads, and has already assembled fifty. Pyongyang's investment in tactical nuclear weapons, hypersonic missiles and submarine-launched capabilities has fuelled concerns in Seoul that nuclear deterrence is giving way to a strategy designed for use in war. The North has also deepened its military ties with Russia, the world's largest nuclear power, allowing its forces to gain valuable combat experience in Ukraine. This is a particularly alarming development for Seoul, because it suggests that Pyongyang's alliance with Moscow is not merely symbolic. Meanwhile, under Kim

Jong-Un's leadership, North Korea has conducted nearly 200 missile tests – almost four times as many as his father and grandfather managed between them over the preceding half-century. Above all, North Korea's newfound ability to strike the United States with intercontinental ballistic missiles (ICBMs) has shaken faith in the American nuclear umbrella. Would a president who puts "America first" and treats alliances as business deals, many South Koreans now ask, really risk San Francisco for Seoul?

If South Korea did decide to cross the nuclear threshold, how would it do so? One option would be for the US to redeploy tactical nuclear weapons to the Korean Peninsula, as it did during the Cold War. At their peak in the 1960s, around 1000 American nuclear warheads were stationed in South Korea – to deter North Korean and communist Chinese military provocations, as well as for use in a nuclear exchange with the Soviet Union – before their removal in 1991. Another possibility would be to establish a NATO-style nuclear-sharing arrangement, allowing South Korea to host or operate US nuclear weapons under joint control. But neither of these options addresses growing doubts about the long-term reliability of America's nuclear umbrella. For this reason, an increasing number of South Koreans support the development of an independent nuclear capability.

Asia is emerging as the new epicentre of nuclear risk

South Korea already possesses a large civilian nuclear energy sector that produces nearly 30 per cent of the country's electricity, alongside a sophisticated missile program that could be adapted for nuclear delivery. It is the only non-nuclear weapons state to operate conventional submarine-launched ballistic missiles, which could provide the foundation for a sea-based deterrent. Professor Lami Kim, an expert on Asia's nuclear politics, suggests it would take at least two to three years for Seoul to build its own bomb. A critical obstacle remains fissile material, the essential ingredient. Without a domestic capacity to produce highly enriched uranium or weapons-grade plutonium, South Korea cannot yet take the final step.

The road to an indigenous arsenal is not without danger for South Korea. Were Seoul to edge closer to the nuclear threshold, the risk of a preventive strike by North Korea may rise. Pyongyang has long made clear that it regards the South's military advancements with deep suspicion. A South Korean nuclear breakout could be seen in the North not only as a threat to the regime but as a justification for military action before the South's arsenal is operational. In a region already rife with miscalculation risks, that possibility cannot be dismissed.

The most serious impediment to South Korea acquiring nuclear weapons may lie not in its technical capacity or the risk of a preventive North Korean attack, but in its alliance with the United States. Under the terms of their 1972 nuclear cooperation agreement – commonly referred to as the "123 Agreement" – Seoul is prohibited from developing uranium enrichment or plutonium reprocessing capabilities, both of which can be used to produce fissile material for nuclear weapons. America has traditionally enforced these restrictions with considerable resolve. It has done so not only to prevent the spread of nuclear weapons, which could erode its military edge and make it harder to deter adversaries, but also to avoid the risk that a nuclear-armed ally, emboldened by its new capabilities, might drag the United States into a war it does not want. In the 1970s, amid talk in Washington of withdrawing US forces and nuclear weapons from the Korean Peninsula, Seoul began exploring the development of its own nuclear capability, including an effort to acquire a reprocessing facility from France. Washington responded by threatening sanctions and warning that such a step would place the entire US–South Korea alliance at risk.

Today, the political landscape has shifted. With Donald Trump in the White House, Seoul may find itself pushing on an open door. During his 2016 presidential campaign, Trump argued that allies such as South Korea and Japan should develop their own nuclear weapons. More recently, Under Secretary of Defense for Policy Elbridge Colby has asserted that South Korea needs to assume primary responsibility for its security because the United States lacks the resources to prepare for war with China while deterring North Korea. Colby has reportedly stated that "all options" should be on the table, including an indigenous South Korean nuclear arsenal.

A South Korean nuclear breakout would pose serious dilemmas for Australia. Canberra and Seoul have grown markedly closer in recent years – not just as fellow US allies but as increasingly aligned Asian middle powers. The two countries, which stood together in the Korean War, upgraded security ties to the level of a Comprehensive Strategic Partnership in December 2021. South Korea is now Australia's fourth-largest trading partner, and cooperation across defence, cyber and critical minerals has deepened significantly.

But a South Korean decision to acquire nuclear weapons would put intense pressure on Australia to choose between competing principles. As a longstanding advocate of the global non-proliferation regime and the rules-based order, Canberra could not easily turn a blind eye. Even if the United States chose to look the other way, other actors – including the European Union, Japan and possibly some of our South-East Asian neighbours – could impose sanctions. Australia, in turn, would come under pressure to follow suit. It would be difficult to justify harsh nuclear sanctions against North Korea while declining to respond to a similar breach by the South. Such inconsistency would expose Canberra to charges of hypocrisy and erode its moral authority on proliferation issues. A nuclear-armed South Korea would, in short, force Australia into a strategic corner, between the preservation of a valued bilateral relationship and fidelity to the non-proliferation regime.

The June 2025 election victory of Democratic Party candidate Lee Jae-myung might offer some short-term reassurance to those worried about South Korea's nuclear ambitions. Progressive presidents like Lee have historically favoured engagement with North

Korea, in contrast to conservatives such as his disgraced predecessor Yoon Suk Yeol, who openly advocated for nuclear weapons. It would be a mistake, however, for Canberra or others to assume the nuclear question is now off the table. The incentives pushing Seoul in this direction – North Korea's growing arsenal, doubts about US reliability, and public support – remain firmly in place. Moreover, previous progressive leaders, such as Roh Moo-hyun and Moon Jae-in, pushed for nuclear-powered submarines – a move that would have required uranium enrichment and edged South Korea even closer to a breakout capability. Their proposals were driven not only by technological ambition but by a deeper impulse: to reduce South Korea's dependence on the United States and to achieve greater autonomy in an increasingly volatile region. For South Korea's progressives, as much as for its conservatives, nuclear weapons may increasingly come to be seen not as an ideological betrayal but as the surest path to long-term security.

A South Korean nuclear breakout would pose serious dilemmas for Australia

Japan: Most capable

If South Korea crosses the nuclear threshold, it is difficult to imagine Japan not following suit. For all the recent efforts by Washington to smooth over tensions between its two North-East Asian allies, deep-seated animosities remain. Japan's brutal colonisation of Korea from 1910 to 1945 continues to cast a shadow and remains a source of friction. Tensions generally resurface most visibly when progressive governments are in power in Seoul, as is now the case. That is because the historical grievance with Japan and the search for justice for past wrongs lies at the heart of progressive foreign policy identity in South Korea. A nuclear-armed South Korea would also confront Japan with the uncomfortable prospect of being left behind in the world's most nuclearised neighbourhood: flanked by the formidable arsenals of China and Russia, and under direct threat from North Korea's increasingly sophisticated and survivable nuclear force.

Even more unsettling for Tokyo is the prospect of Korean unification – especially one that occurs suddenly or that spurs strategic realignment. A unified Korea, particularly if it leans towards China or seeks strategic independence, would mark a profound shift in the Asian balance of power – one that Tokyo could neither ignore nor easily accommodate. Just as calamitous for Tokyo would be a chaotic reunification process that led to the dispersal or theft of North Korea's nuclear assets. In either scenario, Tokyo's longstanding nuclear restraint can no longer be taken for granted.

Japan is widely regarded as one of the world's most advanced threshold nuclear powers. It is sometimes said – only half-jokingly – that it is a mere "screwdriver turn" away from the bomb. While this understates the complexity of nuclear weapons development, Japan's latent capability is undeniable. Nuclear expert Mark Fitzpatrick suggests that it could produce a small atomic arsenal within one to two years if it chose. Tokyo has a sophisticated civilian nuclear energy program, including uranium enrichment facilities and extensive reprocessing capabilities. Indeed, Japan already possesses an estimated 45 tonnes of separated plutonium, which would be sufficient – if further refined – to produce thousands of nuclear warheads. Japan's space launch vehicles and advanced missile programs offer potential delivery platforms, while a range of military aircraft could be adapted to carry nuclear payloads.

Japan's latent nuclear capability has long served a dual strategic purpose: as a hedge against the collapse of American extended deterrence and a source of leverage in alliance diplomacy. Tokyo has rarely played the nuclear card openly, but it has used it skilfully in the past to extract security guarantees and other concessions from Washington. A striking example came in the aftermath of China's first nuclear test, in 1964. Amid growing fears of nuclear coercion and doubts about American resolve, Prime Minister Eisaku Satō's government subtly signalled to Washington that Japan might have no choice but to reconsider its non-nuclear posture. This threat, though never made public, had its intended effect. By simultaneously delaying its signing of the nuclear Non-Proliferation Treaty (NPT) for several years, Tokyo managed to secure firmer US nuclear assurances and the long-sought reversion of Okinawa and other Western Pacific islands that had remained under American administration since the end of World War II.

For decades, this strategy served Japan well. But today it is beginning to fray under the pressure of China's and North Korea's burgeoning nuclear arsenals. The return of Trump has only deepened Tokyo's doubts. The prospect of a prolonged "America First" era may yet force Japan to consider more drastic steps, including the possibility of acquiring nuclear weapons. What once served as a bargaining chip could soon instead become the foundation for a more radical and enduring shift in Japan's defence posture.

The biggest obstacle to Japan taking this path is not technical but political. Unlike in South Korea, where polling consistently shows strong support, roughly the same proportion – around 70 per cent – of the Japanese public favour signing the Treaty on the Prohibition of Nuclear Weapons (TPNW), a far more sweeping rejection of atomic bombs. Such sentiment is deeply grounded in Japan's unique history. Hiroshima and Nagasaki, the only cities ever to suffer a nuclear attack, remain powerful national symbols. For decades, Japan's "Three Non-Nuclear Principles" – no possession, no production and no introduction of nuclear weapons – have remained a cornerstone of its national identity.

Yet it would be a mistake to view Japan's anti-nuclear sentiment as immutable or irreversible. The late prime minister Shinzo Abe signalled a shift in tone as early as 2015, when he controversially omitted mention of the three principles in a speech marking the seventieth anniversary of the Hiroshima bombing. He went further after leaving office, suggesting that Japan should consider NATO-like nuclear-sharing arrangements with the US. In September 2024, Shigeru Ishiba – who soon after became Japan's prime minister – pushed those boundaries further still, telling the Hudson Institute – a prominent American think tank – that he supported the creation of an Asian version of NATO, and that such a body should consider both nuclear sharing with the United States and the introduction of nuclear weapons into the region. That figures of Abe's and Ishiba's stature can express such sentiments publicly suggests that, while Japan's nuclear taboos remain powerful, they are no longer sacrosanct.

The implications of Japan going nuclear would be even more serious for Australia than in the Korean case. Japan is Australia's second-largest trading partner and one of its closest security relationships. Australia and Japan were the chief architects of the "Indo-Pacific" concept, a framing that has been embraced by much of the region and beyond. They have steadily built what both describe as a "Special Strategic Partnership". In 2022, they signed a reciprocal access agreement – allowing each country's forces to train and operate on the other's territory – and updated their joint security declaration using language strikingly like that of the ANZUS Treaty. While not allies in a formal sense, they are intimate enough to be described by analysts in both countries as "quasi-allies".

While Japan's nuclear taboos remain powerful, they are no longer sacrosanct

To be sure, the relationship has not always been smooth. Australia's international legal challenge to Japan's whaling practices and

Tokyo's failed 2016 bid to build Australia's next generation of submarines both left their mark. But the trajectory has been unmistakably one of deepening alignment. Former prime minister Tony Abbott once called Japan Australia's "best friend in Asia" – a sentiment widely shared today in Canberra. That would make any decision to support non-proliferation sanctions against a nuclear-armed Japan even more politically and diplomatically fraught than in the case of South Korea.

Japan is sometimes referred to as the "Britain of Asia" – meaning it is a powerful US ally with significant military capabilities and global diplomatic reach. It is worth remembering that Australia did not object when Britain became the third country to join the nuclear club in the early 1950s. Instead, Canberra directly supported London by supplying uranium and hosting British nuclear tests on Australian soil. Britain was a close ally and a fellow democracy. If the logic then was that it was acceptable, even desirable, for such a trusted partner to possess nuclear weapons, wouldn't the same logic apply to Japan today?

The uncomfortable answer may lie less in principle and more in proximity. A nuclear-armed Britain posed no challenge to Australia's regional position. By contrast, a nuclear-armed Japan would signal a profound loss of faith in the US nuclear umbrella and call into question the credibility of American commitments across the region. This could strain the entire US-led alliance structure and trigger a regional proliferation cascade, hastening the shift towards a more multipolar, less predictable nuclear order in Asia. For all the rhetorical commitment to non-proliferation, Australia's deeper concern may not be with Japan going nuclear but with what Tokyo's decision would reveal: that the old order is passing, including our comfortable place within it.

Indonesia: Most consequential

If Japan were to acquire nuclear weapons, it would reshape Asia's balance of power. If Indonesia did, it would completely transform Australia's strategic outlook. For decades, Australian defence planning has been shadowed by the fear of a hostile Indonesia: a vast, populous nation with very different ethnic and religious foundations. That anxiety reached its apex in the 1960s, when Australia acquired F-111 bombers from the United States, with the expectation – quietly understood in Canberra and Washington – that they could deliver nuclear weapons on Indonesian cities if required.

Today, Indonesia is no adversary. It is a valued partner, a fellow democracy and the central pillar of the Association of Southeast Asian Nations (ASEAN). But the logic of proximity and vulnerability remains. Were Indonesia to pursue nuclear weapons, it would almost certainly trigger a re-evaluation of Australia's non-nuclear posture. As Hugh White put it in his 2019 book, *How to Defend Australia*: "Most of us would take it for granted that the pressure on [Australia] to go nuclear would be vastly amplified if Indonesia went first." A nuclear-armed Indonesia would not just challenge our defence plans. It would force Australia to confront a uniquely acute version of an uncomfortable question: what happens when our Asian friends start thinking about the bomb?

At first glance, the prospect of Indonesia pursuing nuclear weapons seems remote. Jakarta has long positioned itself as a champion of non-proliferation and disarmament. It played a central role in the negotiation of the Southeast Asian Nuclear-Weapon-Free Zone Treaty, which came into force in 1995, and remains one of its most vocal defenders. When AUKUS was unveiled in 2021, Indonesia was quick to stress the importance of Australia's continued adherence to its non-proliferation obligations. Jakarta went further in September 2024 by ratifying the TPNW – a step that few other regional powers, including Australia, have taken.

Yet this principled stance coexists with growing nuclear capacity. Indonesia has deeper experience and infrastructure in nuclear technology than any other South-East Asian nation. In December 2024, its National Energy Council identified twenty-nine potential sites for civilian nuclear power plants, with the first scheduled to come online by 2032. Officially, this effort is framed as a response to intensifying electricity shortfalls and an overreliance on fossil fuels – which still account for around 80 per cent of the country's electricity generation – and the government's commitment to reach net zero emissions by 2060. There are no indications that Jakarta's ambitions extend beyond civilian use.

But capability is not the same as intent, and history reminds us that strategic ambitions can evolve. In a region where nuclear norms are under increasing pressure, today's strategic logic may not hold indefinitely. Indonesia itself offers a telling example. Its fledgling civilian nuclear program began in 1960 with US support under the Atoms for Peace initiative, but by the mid-1960s had taken on a more ominous character. In July 1965, President Sukarno publicly declared Indonesia's desire to acquire nuclear weapons. China had conducted its first successful nuclear test the previous year, and some suspected that Sukarno hoped to leverage the emerging Peking–Jakarta axis to obtain a weapon. Rumours even swirled that a Chinese test might be conducted on one of the thousands of islands in the Indonesian archipelago, allowing Sukarno to claim symbolic entry to the nuclear club. That ambition was short-lived. The transfer of power from Sukarno to Suharto in 1966 marked not only the end of a political era, but the quiet burial of Indonesia's nuclear weapons aspirations – at least for the time being.

Australia has never confronted a challenge like the new nuclear age now unfolding in Asia

Indonesia is on track to become the world's fourth-largest economy by 2050. As its power grows, so will its ambitions. History tells us that rising states tend to translate growing economic weight into military might, and that great powers have typically sought to establish spheres of influence over their immediate region. For many Indonesians, their country is already on the path to becoming an Asian great power. The renowned Australian international relations scholar

Hedley Bull once observed that a nuclear capability is among the defining attributes of great powers. It is not hard to imagine a future Indonesia reaching the same conclusion. Despite its rise, Indonesia's air and naval forces remain relatively underdeveloped, and its economy lags behind those of China and India. In a more contested and dangerous Asia, nuclear weapons could seem to Indonesia's leaders a faster and cheaper route to great-power status, and a potent means of asserting a sphere of influence over its near region.

Australia: On the beach

For more than fifty years, Australia has lived with an uneasy tension in its approach to nuclear weapons. Since ratifying the NPT in 1973, we have pursued two goals simultaneously: discouraging the spread of nuclear weapons, especially in our region, and relying on the protection of America's nuclear umbrella to deter threats we cannot deter alone. On the surface, these aims appear contradictory. Yet they have coexisted – so long as Washington has remained committed to extended deterrence, and so long as our Asian friends, including Japan, South Korea and Indonesia, have refrained from developing nuclear weapons of their own. It is tempting to believe this balancing act can continue. But it won't hold forever. If – or more likely when – those friends cross the nuclear threshold, it will signal that both pillars of Australia's nuclear strategy are giving way. For those countries to go nuclear, they would first need to lose faith in the US umbrella, on which we also depend. Their decisions would mark the failure of the non-proliferation regime we've worked to uphold. That moment may not come in a single instant. But when it does arrive, the unravelling could be faster and more far-reaching than we expect.

Australia has never confronted a challenge like the new nuclear age now unfolding in Asia. Some will argue that the time has come to consider a bomb of our own. It would not be the first time. In the wake of China's first nuclear test, Prime Minister John Gorton's government gave serious thought to acquiring an independent nuclear deterrent. Through the 1970s and into the early 1980s, the Department of Defence quietly kept under review how long it would take to develop such a capability. If it hasn't resumed that practice, it should. Such an assessment needs to include an understanding of the timeline, cost and feasibility of acquiring or producing fissile material, developing or acquiring a delivery system and building the necessary scientific, technical and industrial workforce to support it.

But any decision to pursue nuclear weapons would need to be clear-eyed about the strategic, economic, reputational and moral costs. Geography, which once favoured Australia's defence, now complicates it. Our distance from potential adversaries makes it harder to field a credible nuclear strike capability. We lack the capacity to field ICBMs of the kind China or North Korea could use against us. A nuclear-armed submarine fleet could eventually offer such a capability, but our AUKUS boats remain years away and, at present, are not intended to carry nuclear weapons. Tactical nuclear weapons – smaller warheads intended for use closer to home – might be easier to acquire, but they offer few advantages over conventional capabilities, while carrying disproportionate risks. Any use could invite nuclear retaliation against Australian cities. Even if the United States were to support our acquisition of nuclear weapons – which cannot be assumed – many of our neighbours would strongly oppose it. Acquiring nuclear weapons would breach our obligations under the Treaty of Rarotonga, which underpins the South Pacific Nuclear Free Zone, and likely damage Australia's standing in the parts of the region that matter most: South-East Asia and the South Pacific.

Another option is for Canberra to double down on its non-proliferation efforts, to head off any South Korean, Japanese or Indonesian bid for the bomb. Australia has no shortage of past achievements to draw upon. During the heyday of its middle-power diplomacy in the 1980s and 1990s, Canberra helped to negotiate the South Pacific Nuclear Free Zone Treaty, played a pivotal role in securing the indefinite extension of the NPT, and convened the Canberra Commission on the Elimination of Nuclear Weapons. The government of Kevin Rudd, in partnership with Tokyo, later sponsored the International Commission on Nuclear Non-proliferation and Disarmament.

But that spirit has faded. Over the past two decades, Australian ambition in this space has declined, as has the global appetite for arms control. Much of the architecture that sustained nuclear restraint during the Cold War is crumbling. The 1972 Anti-Ballistic Missile Treaty is gone. So too is the 1987 Intermediate-Range Nuclear Forces Treaty. New START, the last major arms control agreement still in place, has less than a year left to run, with no certainty of renewal. Meanwhile, none of the major nuclear powers has signed the TPNW.

During the Cold War, nuclear strategists talked about two kinds of stability. First, countries needed to believe that building more weapons wouldn't make them safer. This was referred to as "arms race stability". Second, they had to trust that, in a crisis, they wouldn't need to strike first to survive. This was known as "crisis stability". Asia's nuclear future is unlikely to offer either. The region will contain more nuclear-armed states, operating with more varied weapons, doctrines and perceptions of threat. These asymmetries will make arms control harder, because such agreements require at least some sense of parity and mutual restraint. They will also increase the risks of misperception, misjudgement and accidental escalation. Australia's most productive role may lie not in pursuing sweeping arms-control deals, but in helping to reduce the risks of miscalculation and inadvertent nuclear escalation. That means supporting measures such as the establishment and implementation of military-to-military hotlines, crisis communication

Our ability to think strategically about a more nuclear Asia has atrophied

protocols and shared early-warning mechanisms. Wherever possible, these efforts should be advanced in partnership with key regional players – above all, Indonesia – to ensure they reflect regional priorities and carry weight.

Anthony Albanese's government seems to understand these risks and realities. Foreign Minister Penny Wong has consistently warned of the dangers of miscalculation and unintended escalation. Defence Minister Richard Marles has echoed those concerns, as has Prime Minister Albanese. But thus far, rhetoric has outpaced policy. The Department of Foreign Affairs and Trade has reportedly established a new Conflict Prevention and Strategy Branch, but little has been heard of it publicly. Since 2020, Australia has co-chaired a nuclear-risk-reduction workshop with the Philippines under the ASEAN Regional Forum – a body whose record on crisis diplomacy is notoriously lacklustre. While these initiatives are welcome, they are nowhere near enough. If the government is serious about nuclear risk reduction, it will need to invest diplomatic resources, elevate this work in our regional statecraft and do much more to give Canberra's words weight.

One reason Australia has struggled to think clearly about nuclear strategy is that so few in government or beyond it now work seriously on the subject. During the Cold War, nuclear issues were central to strategic thinking, and anyone in the field needed to understand them. Today, they're seen as marginal – a technical niche rather than a strategic priority. As a result, our ability to think strategically about a more nuclear Asia has atrophied. That needs to change. One step would be to rebuild our national expertise. A modest but meaningful start might be a new institute focused on nuclear strategy, policy and proliferation. It might be housed in a leading university or think tank, supported by government, and modelled on overseas efforts – such as the Project on Nuclear Issues (PONI) at Washington's Center for Strategic and International Studies (CSIS), or Harvard's "Managing the Atom" project. It could offer executive education, policy research, regional dialogue and public engagement. If we're going to take nuclear issues seriously again, we'll need more people who understand them.

In his 1957 apocalyptic novel *On the Beach,* Nevil Shute imagined a world in the aftermath of nuclear war, seen from the vantage point of 1960s Melbourne. As the final survivors wait for the radioactive winds to reach them, they know what's coming but are powerless to stop it. Shute's story – which became a major Hollywood film starring Gregory Peck and Ava Gardner – struck a chord because it captured something deeply human: our reluctance to confront uncomfortable truths until it's too late.

Australia doesn't yet face nuclear catastrophe. But we do confront the end of a nuclear order that has served us well, and the beginning of something far more dangerous. A new era of nuclear risk is already taking shape in our region. The American nuclear umbrella and the non-proliferation regime we've relied on are fraying. Our closest friends and partners might build the bomb. For too long we have avoided thinking seriously about nuclear weapons. That is no longer sustainable. If those closest to us are preparing for a darker nuclear future, we need to talk about how we might survive in it. We're not yet living in Nevil Shute's world. But unless we begin to reckon with these questions, we may find ourselves in it. ■

BEYOND AUKUS

Could Australia get the bomb?

Stephan Frühling & Andrew O'Neil

Nuclear weapons continue to cast a shadow across international relations. The fraying of arms control, Russia's nuclear threats in its war against Ukraine, and rapid Chinese and North Korean expansion of their arsenals are throwing up uncomfortable questions for non-nuclear powers. Donald Trump's rhetoric accusing US allies of freeriding is adding to this discomfort, as is his incoherent approach to dealing with Russia and China. Many US allies in North-East Asia and Europe are becoming jittery about the robustness of US nuclear guarantees and are flirting with alternatives.

In North-East Asia, Japanese anxieties over the credibility of the US nuclear umbrella continue to percolate, with some senior figures noting publicly that Tokyo might review its non-proliferation commitments. Japan's possession of significant stocks of plutonium and its long-range strike and space launch vehicle capabilities mean that it would be well positioned to become a fully-fledged nuclear weapons state, should it decide to go down this path.

South Korean politicians and commentators continue to signal their unease over the credibility of the American nuclear umbrella. In recent years, South Korea has developed a significant missile program, and while it does not have a plutonium reprocessing facility, its nuclear industry comprises a large number of power reactors and the ability to produce more.

In Europe, which is experiencing its largest war since 1945, France and the United Kingdom have confirmed they will coordinate their nuclear arsenals in responding to major threats, while also signalling the extension of their nuclear umbrella to European allies. Poland has indicated an interest in exploring a greater role in the NATO nuclear deterrent, and hinted at possibly developing a nuclear weapons program of its own. Meanwhile, the United Kingdom is returning the Royal Air Force to the nuclear mission, acquiring F-35As to rejoin NATO's "nuclear sharing", under which the United States provides nuclear gravity bombs for delivery by allied aircraft.

Should we also be asking whether Australia needs to consider accessing nuclear weapons for our long-term security?

Nuclear weapons are the ultimate deterrent because of the unmatched scale and speed of their destructive impact. Australia has placed deterrence at the core of its defence policy since 2020, when concern about China's strategic behaviour began to spike. Bipartisan commitment to acquire nuclear-powered submarines under AUKUS recognises that fundamentally new capabilities will be required to defend Australia. A surprising 36 per cent of Australians were in favour of acquiring nuclear weapons in the 2022 Lowy Poll, a large jump from 16 per cent in 2010 (although even back then, 42 per cent of respondents were only in favour of doing so if a neighbouring country acquired them).

The received wisdom about the spread of nuclear weapons is that proliferation triggers a domino effect, whereby states would acquire the bomb in response to others doing so. The Treaty on the Non-Proliferation of Nuclear Weapons (NPT), coupled with the growth of increasingly robust International Atomic Energy Agency (IAEA) safeguards, has undoubtedly slowed the pace of proliferation over the past fifty-five years. Only Israel, Pakistan, India and North Korea have joined the five "declared" nuclear powers codified in the NPT. This is an average of one new nuclear-armed state every fourteen years, a long way from the widespread predictions in the 1960s that the world could have twenty-five to thirty nuclear-armed states by 2000.

But the popular "domino theory" is unconvincing. North Korea, Iran, Iraq, Syria and Libya – all of which have had active nuclear weapons programs following the Cold War – sought the bomb because of their relative conventional weakness, not nuclear threats. Would South Korea, Taiwan, Poland or even Sweden acquiring nuclear weapons tip, say, Germany, Japan or Australia into following suit? It is more likely that attempts by an unrestrained Moscow or Beijing to impose their hegemony on Eurasia would lead countries with similar outlooks to react in a similar way. The question then is: if Japan or South Korea seek their own bomb, would Australia necessarily take the same step?

Australia and nuclear weapons

Australia has flirted with acquiring nuclear weapons in the past, during previous bouts of concern about the reliability of the United States as an ally. In the 1960s, allied confidence in US security guarantees was severely shaken by the new Kennedy administration. Washington's rejection of the nuclear strategy of "massive retaliation" in favour of "flexible response" – and in particular Secretary of Defense Robert McNamara's belief that this would entail a much-reduced role for nuclear weapons in the defence of NATO – raised existential fears in Europe about US commitment. West Germany and Italy toyed with developing nuclear weapons alongside the French, while US policy reinforced President Charles de Gaulle's mistrust in the credibility of extended deterrence, and his determination that France develop an independent *force de frappe*.

In Australia, similar fears manifested as China acquired the bomb in 1964, and Washington refused to provide guarantees of support during *Konfrontasi* with Indonesia. A sovereign nuclear weapons program came to be seen as a potential alternative to the alliance with the United States, as Washington increasingly seemed unwilling or unable to commit to defending Australia's security. In a 1966 National Intelligence Estimate, US agencies assessed that if Australia concluded that the US was being pushed out of South-East Asia, "the chances are about even that it would develop its own nuclear weapons".

In the late 1960s, backing an Australian nuclear force was not a fringe political or strategic position. Those sympathetic to the cause included the chair of the Atomic Energy Commission, Sir Philip Baxter, the country's leading physicist, Sir Ernest Titterton, and several Liberal and Democratic Labor Party politicians, including the Minister for National Development, David Fairbairn. When John Gorton's coalition government drew up plans to build a nuclear reactor at Jervis Bay in 1969, part of the agenda was to develop a pathway to the bomb.

Research from this time examined the ideal technical attributes and the funding required for a fully-fledged inventory that included intercontinental ballistic missiles (ICBMs) carrying a significant number of nuclear warheads. These musings faded after Australia signed the NPT in 1970 and following the cancellation of the Jervis Bay nuclear reactor project in 1971. But for more than a decade the Australian government considered that it may one day need the bomb, and the Defence Department continued to recommend pegging acquisition times to the capabilities of countries in the region, particularly Indonesia. In his memoirs, former foreign minister Bill Hayden recounts how he recommended to a small group of Hawke government colleagues that Australia retain the technical capacity to achieve a threshold nuclear weapons capability; it was not until 1987 that nuclear switches and wiring were removed from Australia's F-111 strike aircraft.

The idea of an Australian bomb has never really gone away

The idea of an Australian bomb as an alternative to relying on the US alliance has never really gone away. That Australian governments have not (yet) revisited Gorton's thinking is due to various factors, including international treaty commitments, domestic and global norms opposing proliferation, technical hurdles, and assurances provided by the US alliance, most notably extended nuclear deterrence. The latter was recognised obliquely in the 2009 Defence White Paper, which referred to "the stable and reliable sense of assurance" provided by the US nuclear umbrella, which "has removed the need for Australia to consider more significant and expensive defence options".

The most prominent recent analysis of whether Australia should consider nuclear weapons appeared in Hugh White's 2019 book, *How to Defend Australia*. White's argument is that as confidence in America's ability to defend its Indo-Pacific allies against China declines, so will allies' confidence in US commitments, including nuclear deterrence. From this perspective, Beijing's capacity to strike the continental United States with a nuclear payload – even after having absorbed a first strike – will inevitably deter Washington from following through on its declared commitment to the nuclear umbrella. For White, waning confidence in the credibility of nuclear deterrence triggers a stark question for Australia: do we need a nuclear weapon of our own to deter Chinese nuclear threats against Australia in a conventional war?

Were Australia to go down the proliferation pathway, White believes, the only viable option would be to acquire a minimum deterrent force along the lines of that possessed by the United Kingdom, which would allow Australia to retaliate against a Chinese first strike: "We would need a stockpile of a couple of hundred sophisticated [thermonuclear] weapons, a fleet of at least four ballistic missile-firing submarines (which would have to be nuclear-powered to ensure their survival), and the ballistic missiles to go in them." Yet, for political and practical reasons, there remain significant doubts about whether Australia could produce such an advanced capability at the scale necessary and within the time required to address rapid strategic change.

Anti-nuclear nation

Since the 1940s, Australia has viewed a strong alliance with the United States as the optimal means of achieving protection against existential threats. In addition, the costs of developing adequate weapons technology separate from the US alliance were seen as excessive. Australia places value on being "self-reliant" in the defence of Australia and in the ability of the Australian Defence Force (ADF) to operate independently if required, and has regarded cultivating security partnerships in the Indo-Pacific as the best way to mitigate risks.

Of these tenets of Australian strategic policy, only the last would seem to militate against Australia acquiring nuclear weapons. Such a move by Canberra could risk rupturing our relationship with ASEAN and severely compromising our leadership role in the Pacific.

Acquisition of nuclear weapons by South Korea and Japan would spell a de facto, if not de jure, end to the NPT. However, Australia would still be bound by the South Pacific Nuclear Free Zone Treaty, which forbids the transfer or possession of nuclear weapons and which, for South Pacific nations, is grounded in memories of colonial exploitation as sites of nuclear testing. Australia acquiring nuclear weapons – no matter the circumstances – would be, to say the least, unwelcome in our neighbourhood. The adverse impact on the relationship with Australia's most important regional neighbour, Indonesia, could also trigger a reassessment in Jakarta of its own non-nuclear status.

Australia's strategic policy also reflects its political norms. Unlike in Japan and South Korea, no serious political or social figure in Australia today advocates acquiring nuclear weapons. Australians have mixed views about nuclear issues: while a clear majority favour Australia acquiring nuclear-powered submarines as part of AUKUS, the 2025 federal election showed that proposals to build civilian nuclear power capacity in Australia struggle to gain public support. It seems inconceivable that any Australian government could embark on a decades-long program to acquire and operate nuclear weapons without the idea receiving bipartisan support.

Since the 1970s, successive governments have cultivated a profile for Australia as a responsible global citizen that adheres to international law and norms. This has been reflected in Australia's activism on global issues – including non-proliferation and arms control – in multilateral forums. For many, including those from the left wing of the Labor Party, a big component of Australia's reputation as a responsible global citizen is its support for nuclear disarmament.

More broadly, Australia has played a hands-on role in strengthening the nuclear non-proliferation regime through its membership of export control groups and its support for inspection and safeguard initiatives (including the IAEA's development of the Additional Protocol), and by being a model non-nuclear-weapons state in contributing to advances in non-proliferation technologies in the Indo-Pacific. Australia's efforts to promote transparency around its negotiations with the IAEA to strengthen safeguards to verify that Australia is not diverting nuclear material transferred under AUKUS to weapons programs should be seen in this light. Australia's strong historical support for non-proliferation reflects the reality that we would have a lot to lose from further proliferation in the Indo-Pacific.

For an Australian government to decide to acquire the bomb, this framework would need to have broken down. This is not beyond the bounds of possibility: established norms evolve and sometimes even disappear. In response to Russia's aggression in Europe, Germany's Greens Party, for example, has become one of the staunchest advocates of increased defence spending and nuclear sharing, a world of difference from its origins in the West German peace movement of the 1980s. Nevertheless, only an unprecedented shift in Australia's strategic and political perspective, triggered by a serious external shock – such as China conquering Taiwan, or Washington openly and unequivocally walking away from a key alliance, especially with Japan – could prompt it to reconsider its commitment to non-proliferation.

An Australian Manhattan Project?

Technically speaking, what would it take for Australia to acquire nuclear weapons?

Three capabilities are required for the development of nuclear weapons. The first is to produce fissile materials: uranium can be "enriched" to 90 per cent of the uranium-239 isotope, while plutonium can be reprocessed from uranium that has been irradiated in a nuclear reactor. The plutonium route requires bigger and more expensive infrastructure, but allows the building of lightweight and compact warheads with higher yields. A reactor is also needed for producing the hydrogen isotope tritium, which is required for more advanced warhead designs.

The second required capability encompasses weapon design, triggering mechanisms and testing instrumentation for the warhead. The third is a delivery vehicle appropriate for the way the weapon is intended to be used; this could be as simple as a buried nuclear landmine. If a long-range missile capable of carrying a nuclear payload was to be developed from scratch, this would probably take longer than the fabrication of the warheads themselves.

Australia has considerable commercial uranium mining, but has no reactor suitable to produce plutonium, nor any expertise in reactor design and construction. But we do possess expertise in uranium enrichment. The Australian company Silex leads the world in the development of new laser-enrichment technology, a technology so proliferation-sensitive that in the late 1990s the Howard government felt it necessary to sign an agreement to share the technology with the United States. Laser enrichment continues to be co-developed for commercial purposes at the Lucas Heights facility in Sydney. Australia also operated an experimental uranium centrifuge plant at Lucas Heights until the 1980s, the technical information from which remains in the custody of the Australian Nuclear Science and Technology Organisation (ANSTO).

Hence, Australia has some experience, even if it is now largely in documentary form, of the technical challenges of running centrifuges, such as producing sufficiently pure uranium hexafluoride gas. While early centrifuge rotors were made from maraging steel, modern ones are made from carbon fibre, a technology in which Australia has longstanding R&D and industrial capabilities. In general, the specialised technologies required to produce centrifuges include clean rooms, vacuum pumps, high-precision lathes, autoclaves, metal etching, magnets and precision measurement. Australian universities and the aeronautics and defence industry sectors have experience with most, if not all, of these dual-use technologies, and access to equipment that is often export-controlled.

Australia has played a hands-on role in strengthening the nuclear non-proliferation regime

Technologies required for building the nuclear warhead include theoretical physics for the design, explosive lenses, high-speed and precision triggers and detonators, a neutron source, diagnostic equipment for detonators and neutron flux, precision lathing, and beryllium metal production. Again, Australian industry and, in particular, universities house much of the relevant physical, chemical and engineering expertise and equipment. Nuclear physics research has been part of the Australian National University (ANU) since its creation in 1946. High-precision measuring is a capability well developed in universities, and instrumentation for the heavy ion accelerator facility at ANU – as well as ANSTO's research reactor – also gives Australia solid expertise in nuclear measurements. Australia's advanced precision-engineering industry is also relevant, including metallurgy and foundries, computer-controlled lathes and some companies that work to accuracies measured in micrometres or nanometres.

Would Australia build a bomb?

So Australia could build a bomb if it really wanted to, although not as easily as Japan or South Korea. The real question concerns trade-offs.

A "crash program" – where Australia prioritises the rapid development of its own nuclear weapons – would require huge political capital to justify, which might put at risk domestic support and international partnerships essential to adjusting to the new regional security environment. Australia would need to devote scarce scientific, industrial and fiscal resources to prioritising investment in nuclear over conventional weapons. And the country would need to consider the costs and benefits of a program that might only produce a handful of fission warheads and would take decades to develop a credible intercontinental strike capability akin to that of established nuclear powers.

Even a less-restrained China would likely need time to digest Taiwan, to subdue Japan and perhaps South Korea and Southeast Asia. In such circumstances, it is unlikely that Australia would find itself at the top of Beijing's geopolitical hit list. That could buy us the additional breathing space we might need, compared to, for example, Japan or South Korea.

But a handful of fission warheads – which is all a crash program could hope to achieve – would be of limited practical use. It would be a far cry from the robust arsenal Hugh White writes about, and at best yield a capability that might only be useful in sinking a few ships along Australia's approaches. And what better way would there be of bringing us into Beijing's crosshairs than starting a nuclear program while remaining vulnerable to major conventional attack?

There are strong arguments against Australia developing its own nuclear weapons in response to rapid strategic change, even if Japan or South Korea were to do so. One of these is that even if the NPT had broken apart, Australia would still be bound by its non-proliferation commitments under the Rarotonga Treaty. Also, it would require massive and unprecedented investment for Australia to gain the technology to operationalise a nuclear force. Even then, it would take many years, during which rapidly building up our conventional military strength would have to be the overwhelming priority. As political scientist Vipin

Narang has observed, "Strong consensus among key domestic constituencies is necessary to push states onto the path of active nuclear pursuit." Australia is no South Korea, Japan, France or even Sweden, with national trust and pride in its technological and industrial capabilities. Defence Minister David Johnston's 2014 comment that he wouldn't trust the Australian-government owned defence industry company ASC "to build a canoe" epitomises an attitude widely shared among the political class.

Technically speaking, Australia could build a bomb, but the notion that it would do so quickly as an alternative to the US alliance makes little strategic or political sense.

AUKUS, the alliance and the bomb

Achieving greater self-reliance to replace the US alliance might not be the only reason Australia decides to seek a nuclear capability. Seeking access to nuclear weapons has also been seen by countries – including Australia in the 1950s and 1960s – as a way of strengthening, renewing and renegotiating alliances with major powers. In Europe, the United States continues to "share" nuclear warheads for delivery by the aircraft of several NATO allies: an arrangement the Trump administration insists will continue even if the US reduces its conventional forces in Europe. "Nuclear burden sharing" of the financial and political cost of nuclear deterrence, as well as of the strategic risk of nuclear war, is an underlying principle of NATO's approach, which the Americans have yet to demand of their allies in the Indo-Pacific.

Even the French example of a sovereign and independent nuclear force is less a rejection than a renegotiation of the alliance relationship: President de Gaulle withdrew France from most (although not all) military integration with NATO, but did not leave NATO, let alone abrogate France's alliance with the United States. And the United Kingdom's nuclear forces remain deeply integrated with those of the United States: Britain's warheads are a variant of the US W76 design, and its nuclear submarine-launched missiles are drawn from a shared stock with the US Navy, an arrangement that will continue with the new US Constellation and UK Dreadnought missile submarine classes, currently under construction. This arrangement dates to the 1958 US–UK Mutual Defence Agreement, under which the United States first agreed to share its nuclear submarine propulsion technology with the United Kingdom. In effect, this arrangement has been renewed and expanded to involve Australia through AUKUS.

AUKUS raises questions about nuclear proliferation, but not in the way that its critics typically maintain

We should not assume, therefore, that Australia would only contemplate acquiring nuclear weapons as an alternative to the US alliance. Instead, acquiring nuclear weapons could be a continuation, perhaps even a strengthening, of the alliance if the Americans decided they did not wish to carry the burden of security commitments in North-East Asia. The prospect of South Korea and Japan acquiring nuclear weapons in these circumstances would increase considerably. Both are frontline states directly exposed to the full force of China's military, and the domestic pressures to go nuclear in response to Chinese aggression would be intense. For Australia, geographically removed from China's potential sphere of influence in North-East Asia, the pressure to acquire nuclear weapons would be less acute. Still, Australian policymakers would be concerned about the heightened prospects of Chinese coercion, especially if Taiwan were conquered.

The Trump administration could move to an offshore balancing strategy over the next three years, by which Washington would avoid playing an active role in local conflicts but would support regional powers to balance China. As Stephen Walt notes, this strategy is predicated on the United States not needing to control vital areas directly; it only has to ensure that they did not fall under the control of peer competitors.

Offshore balancing would likely spell the end of the United States' alliances with Japan and South Korea – but would it necessarily spell the end of its Australian alliance? Australia has always argued that the alliance is a net benefit for the Americans rather than a burden: Australia has fought in all major US conflicts since World War I, hosts US forces and joint facilities, and participates both in the exclusive "Five Eyes" intelligence network and (since 2021) in the "Anglo club" of AUKUS.

There are also sound arguments that the United States would regard Australia's relevance for its security differently from that of its other allies. These other allies are all located in what Nicholas J. Spykman, in his 1944 book *The Geography of the Peace*, called the "rimlands" of Eurasia: a zone that can be contested by the world's global maritime power, currently the United States, and by the big land powers of Eurasia. By contrast, the Australian continent, which lies beyond the South-East Asian archipelago, is geostrategically one of the "outer lying islands": Canberra is further from Beijing than is Berlin, after all. Any Eurasian power posing an existential threat to Australia would demonstrate hegemonic ambitions on a scale that would also threaten the United States, even if it had withdrawn to Guam, Alaska and Hawaii.

American strategists have long thought in these terms, and would continue to do so if the United States reduced its broader commitments in the Indo-Pacific. General Douglas MacArthur commented during World War II that Australia was relevant to the United States because of its geographical position, not because of the people inhabiting the continent. Australia will always be an important base area on the southern flank of a possible threat to Hawaii. Geographically, all "Five Eyes" countries are relevant for the defence of the Western Hemisphere: Canada, which covers the northern approaches; Britain, which anchors the defences of the US eastern seaboard, across the UK–Iceland–Greenland gap, and Australia and New Zealand, as a southern bulwark from which to defend the wide expanse of the Pacific.

It seems certain that Australia would continue advancing these same ideas about the geographic basis of its own strategic relevance, especially in a situation of uncertainty and upheaval. The alternative – a small country of 28 million going it alone and eschewing whatever US support and commitment might still be available in a reordered Indo-Pacific – would be even more uncertain, and possibly catastrophic.

In that sense, AUKUS raises questions about nuclear proliferation, but not in the way that its critics typically maintain – that Australia might be tempted to divert the enriched uranium from its future nuclear-powered submarines to a dedicated weapons program. Instead, if Washington embraces Australia's role as the southern anchor in an offshore balancing strategy, AUKUS could open the door to a transfer of nuclear weapons technology from the United States to Australia: an expansion of AUKUS to extend it to the full range of US–UK nuclear cooperation, which began in 1958. In a world in which the United States might leave its former allies in the "rimlands" to their own devices in the face of Chinese hegemonic ambitions, the idea of Australia, the United Kingdom and the United States once more redefining their relationship – this time as allied (nuclear) powers guarding their shared maritime approaches – seems no more far-fetched than Australia striking out on its own with an antipodean version of the Manhattan Project. ■

THE CHALLENGE

Reviving nuclear arms control diplomacy

Gareth Evans

Nuclear arms control has never been more necessary, and never more difficult to achieve. In all three of its dimensions – risk reduction, non-proliferation and outright elimination – the outlook ranges from desolate to hopeless. The important arms control agreements of the past are dead, dying or on life support. And the recent behaviour of the actors that matter most – the United States, Russia and China – has fed concerns that things can only get worse.

The nine nuclear-armed states possess between them over 12,200 nuclear warheads, with a combined destructive capacity of more than 145,000 Hiroshima bombs. Some 9000 of these are militarily active or deployed. Alarmingly, some 2000 US and Russian weapons remain on high alert, ready to be launched within a decision window for each president of four to eight minutes. The US and Russia, holding between them 90 per cent of the global stockpile, dramatically downsized their inventories after the end of the Cold War, but that momentum has completely stalled. Every nuclear-armed state is now modernising or increasing its arsenal, especially China, whose inventory has doubled in a few short years to nearly 600 weapons, with new land- and seaborne delivery systems.

More troubling still, the longstanding taboo against the use of nuclear weapons seems to be weakening, with Russia's President Vladimir Putin in particular talking up this prospect in the Ukraine war in language not heard since the height of the Cold War. A number of states are considering using nuclear weapons – especially so-called "tactical" weapons – not just for deterrence but for warfighting.

The big arms control agreements of the past, which – at least between the US and Russia – banned certain systems outright, set constraints on deployments and built confidence through transparency, are now either dead (the Anti-Ballistic Missile, Intermediate-range Nuclear Forces and Open Skies treaties) or dying (the 2010 Strategic Arms Reduction Treaty [New START]). If, as seems likely, the latter expires in February 2026, Russia and the US will be without any limits on their nuclear forces for the first time in over fifty years.

Moreover, crucial multilateral treaties are on life support. The Comprehensive Nuclear-Test-Ban Treaty (CTBT), though operating in practice, has still not been finally ratified. And the Treaty on the Non-Proliferation of Nuclear Weapons (NPT) is in as fragile a condition as it has ever been. The loss of confidence in Washington's willingness to deliver on its extended nuclear – or even conventional – deterrence commitment to close allies has led to serious discussion in South Korea, and even in some quarters in Japan, about the need to acquire their own nuclear weapons. The US strikes against Iran's nuclear sites, without any pretence of a legally defensible imminent threat to Israel or anyone else, seems as likely as not to finally convince Tehran's leaders that actually building bombs is their best chance of survival. And any such move is bound to be contagious. The belief that Ukraine would not be in the trouble it is if it had not given back its Soviet-era weapons remains widespread.

The safeguards system of the International Atomic Energy Agency (IAEA) is still reasonably functional, as are less formal restraint mechanisms such as the Nuclear Suppliers Group and Missile Technology Control Regime. About the only other good news on the non-proliferation agreement front is that regional nuclear-weapon-free zone (NWFZ) treaties are continuing to hold their own in South-East Asia (with China recently, at long last, agreeing to join), the South Pacific, Latin America, Africa and the Antarctic.

Nuclear disarmament discussion has become more complicated in recent years

While there is less to it than meets the eye, the Treaty on the Prohibition of Nuclear Weapons (TPNW), agreed by 122 UN member states in 2017 and in force since 2021, bans nuclear weapons outright, and has given new heart to anti-nuclear campaigners. But there is no prospect, for the foreseeable future, of this being signed or ratified by the states that matter –the nuclear-armed states, or the "umbrella" states (like Australia) believing themselves to be sheltering under their protection. Moreover, nuclear disarmament discussion has become more complicated in recent years with ever more dual-use systems in operation, especially ballistic or cruise missiles which could carry either nuclear or conventional weapons, and the emergence of real concerns about the development of weapons in space, hypersonic weapons, lethal autonomous weapons, cyberwarfare and the impact of AI generally. Multilateral agreements for most of these new areas have barely been even conceptualised, let alone negotiated.

For all the difficulties that confront the cause of nuclear arms control, it must never be abandoned. The starting point is for policymakers and those who influence them to understand – or be reminded, if they have forgotten – why this matters so much.

Making the case

The *moral* case – for not just reducing the risk of nuclear weapons use but eliminating them entirely from the world's arsenal – is compellingly simple. They are the most indiscriminately inhumane weapons ever devised. The almost indescribable horror associated with nuclear weapon use informed the first resolution of the UN General Assembly, in 1946, and has been at the heart of all disarmament advocacy since.

Moreover, their full-scale use in a nuclear war would threaten the existence of life on this planet as we know it. The "nuclear winter" impact of a major nuclear exchange, even one confined to a single region like South Asia, would be globally devastating. With millions of tons of smoke lofted to high altitude and absorbing sunlight, surface temperatures and precipitation would dramatically fall, threatening a significant fraction of the world's food supply, and such "nuclear famine" would put at risk the lives of nearly a billion people.

The *legal* case – if not for total abolition, at least for banning the threat or use of nuclear weapons in all but the most extreme and exceptional circumstances – is also compelling. The 1996 Advisory Opinion of the International Court of Justice on the *Legality of the Threat or Use of Nuclear Weapons* (I appeared in the case as advocate for Australia) decided unanimously that "[t]here is in neither customary nor conventional international law any specific authorization of the threat or use of nuclear weapons"; and by seven votes to seven (with the president's casting vote) that "the threat or use of nuclear weapons would generally be contrary to the rules of international law applicable in armed conflict and in particular the principles and rules of humanitarian law". Although the court added that it "cannot conclude definitively whether the threat or use of nuclear weapons would be lawful or unlawful in an extreme circumstance of self-defence, in which the very survival of a State would be at stake", it follows from its opinion that there is no circumstance in which a state can be sure that its use of nuclear weapons will be lawful. Their use plainly is unlawful in most circumstances – and may well be unlawful in all circumstances.

The *rational* case for a nuclear-weapon-free world matters more than any legal or even moral argument. Hard-headed policymakers unashamedly argue that the sheer awfulness of nuclear weapons is what makes them so effective as a deterrent. They need to be persuaded of the force of the practical strategic arguments against nuclear weapons: that the rewards for their possession are illusory, and far outweighed by the risks.

The illusion of reward

Nuclear weapons are at best of minimal, and at worst of zero, utility in maintaining peace, whether the context be deterring war between large nuclear-armed powers or protecting weaker states against conventional attack.

It is too often accepted as self-evident that the balance of nuclear terror between the United States and the Soviet Union maintained peace throughout the Cold War – and has been important since in restraining other potential belligerents (including India and Pakistan, India and China, China and the US, and – in the context of the Ukraine conflict – NATO and Russia) from going to war with each other. But this argument is not nearly as strong as it might seem.

While of course "mutually assured destruction" (MAD) encouraged a degree of caution in how the Soviet Union and US approached each other, there is no evidence that at any time either side wanted to initiate war and was constrained from doing so only by the existence of the other side's nuclear weapons.

We know that knowledge of an adversary's possession of supremely destructive weapons (as with chemical and biological weapons before 1939) has not stopped war between major powers. Nor has the experience or prospect of massive damage to cities and civilian death tolls caused leaders to back down – including after the bombing of Hiroshima and Nagasaki. There is strong evidence that the key factor driving Japan to sue for peace was not the nuclear attacks; it was the Soviet Union's declaration of war later that same week.

But if nuclear weapons have not preserved the "Long Peace" since 1945, what has? A plausible explanation is simply that the major powers realised, after the experience of World War II (and given the rapid technological advances that followed), that the damage inflicted by *any* war between them would be unbelievably horrific, far outweighing any conceivable benefit.

Nuclear weapons are at best of minimal, and at worst of zero, utility in maintaining peace

What of the notion, more immediately relevant to today's Ukraine and Iran, that nuclear weapons are a strategic equaliser, necessary to compensate for inferior conventional capabilities? North Korea certainly seems to believe that possession of even a small number of nuclear weapons constitutes a deterrent against forcible regime change, with the experience of Serbia in 1999, Iraq in 2003, Libya in 2011 and now Iran in 2025 no doubt reinforcing the perception that states without such weapons are vulnerable to attack.

But weapons that would be manifestly suicidal to use are not ultimately a very credible deterrent. Their retention by Ukraine after the break-up of the Soviet Union would not have stopped Russia's invasion, because Moscow knows that Kyiv would be no more likely than any of the NATO nuclear powers to nuke Moscow in response to a conventional attack: the risk of nuclear retaliation would simply be too great. A better deterrent for North Korea against any likely attack (and I have been told by some Chinese analysts in a position to know, albeit some years ago, that the Pyongyang leadership actually believes this, however much they enjoy their nuclear show) is its hugely formidable "ring of fire" artillery and rocket placements within close range of Seoul.

Despite the psychological comfort they give their possessors, nuclear weapons are not the stabilising tools they are commonly assumed to be. Conflicts have regularly occurred in which nuclear weapons could have played a part but did not. Consider the long list of wars in which non-nuclear powers either directly attacked nuclear powers or were not deterred by the prospect of their nuclear intervention: Korea, Vietnam, Yom Kippur, Falklands, the two in Afghanistan since the 1970s, and the first Gulf War.

Then there are the cases where both sides' possession of nuclear weapons, rather than operating as a constraint, has given one side the opportunity to launch small military actions without serious fear of nuclear reprisal, owing to the too-high stakes of such a response. The Kargil War between Pakistan and India in 1999 is an example, as perhaps are this year's hostilities over Kashmir. There is substantial quantitative as well as anecdotal evidence to support the "stability/instability paradox" – the notion that what may appear to be a stable nuclear balance actually encourages more violence. The old conservative line is that "the absence of nuclear weapons would make the world safe for conventional wars". But it may, rather, be the *presence* of nuclear weapons that has made the world safer for such wars.

If the cause of disarmament is to gain momentum, the nuclear-armed states – and those who shelter beneath them – will have to be persuaded that their security will not be prejudiced by relying on conventional weaponry rather than on inherently unusable weapons of mass destruction, and above all on intelligent, cooperative-security-focused diplomacy. It is not hard to make that argument rationally; the biggest hurdles will always be psychological, emotional and political.

The reality of risk

The strongest argument for the outright elimination of nuclear weapons is the enormous risks involved in their continued possession by anybody. As compellingly stated by those quintessential Cold War realists Henry Kissinger, George Shultz, Bill Perry and Sam Nunn in their famous series of *Wall Street Journal* articles from 2007 onwards, whatever may have been the case in the past, in today's world those risks far outweigh any conceivable security returns.

The risks that the "four horsemen" (and many others) have identified go not so much to aggressive first use of nuclear weapons – though it simply cannot be assumed that calm, considered rationality will always prevail in the enormous stress of a real-time crisis. The prospect of a complete madman's finger on the trigger may be more fictional than real, but what cannot be discounted is the possibility of an impetuous, ill-informed and unconstrained leader ordering a "minimal" strike, maybe in misconceived pursuit of an "escalate to de-escalate" strategy, with all the chance of the situation spiralling out of control that would entail.

The bigger risk is stumbling into a catastrophe through accident, human error, system error or sabotage. Throughout the Cold War, and particularly after 1960, when the US first deployed an early-warning system, there was – as comprehensively listed by the Federation of American Scientists in *The Washington Post* in June 2025 – an almost unbelievable series of falsely reported attacks which could easily have resulted in nuclear Armageddon, had there not in each case happened to be at least one or two cool heads in the room, prepared to wait for confirmation before triggering a reflex response. Among them, alarms of incoming missile barrages have been triggered in the US by a military exercise tape being mistakenly fed into the live warning system (in 1979) and by the failure of a single computer chip (in 1980, twice), and in the Soviet Union by the misreading of sunlight on high-altitude clouds (in 1983).

Potentially devastating mishaps have continued to occur in the post–Cold War years, not only involving the two nuclear superpowers. In 1995 Russian president Boris Yeltsin was advised to retaliate immediately against an incoming NATO missile, which proved to be a Norwegian scientific rocket. In 2007 the US Air Force mistakenly loaded six live-armed cruise missiles on a B-52 bomber, flew them cross-country and left them unguarded for a day with nobody noticing. In 2022 an errant Ukrainian missile landing in Poland was for hours mistaken for a Russian weapon deliberately targeting a NATO ally. In 2022, again, an Indian missile crashed into Pakistani territory – it was the result of human error by the launch crew but, in the absence of any explanation or communication between military leaders, triggered a high-alert response. In the most recent conflict between the two subcontinental nuclear powers, in May 2025, Indian drones went close to triggering a nuclear crisis by attacking a site very close to a key hub in Pakistan's nuclear command and control system.

Given what we now know about the Cold War United States–Soviet Union near misses and that we now have seven other nuclear-armed states compounding the danger; given what we know about the rather more uncertain command and control and mutual reassurance systems of the more recently nuclear-armed states; and given also what we now know, and can guess, about how much more sophisticated and capable cyber offence will be of overcoming cyber defence in the years ahead, the fact that we have survived for eight decades without a nuclear weapons catastrophe is not a matter of inherent system stability or great statesmanship – just sheer dumb luck. And there is no reason why that luck should continue indefinitely.

The Australia-initiated Canberra Commission on the Elimination of Nuclear Weapons, in its 1996 report, stated the case for outright abolition with admirable succinctness: "So long as any state retains nuclear weapons, others will want them. So long as any nuclear weapons remain anywhere, they are bound one day to be used – if not by design, then by human error, system error, miscalculation or misjudgement. And any such use will be catastrophic for life on this planet as we know it."

The challenge of elimination

Despite the force of these arguments, none of the existing nuclear-armed states have shown the slightest willingness to give up their nuclear weapons. The testosterone factor – considerations of status, prestige and nuclear bragging rights, whether rationally well founded or not – continues to be in play for most, if not all, of them. And the optimism associated with the end of the Cold War has long since evaporated, with little or no sign now – among policymakers, publics or commentariats – of the abolitionist momentum captured by the Reagan–Gorbachev Reykjavík statement in 1987 that "a nuclear war cannot be won and must never be fought".

Russia's aggression, America's wavering commitment, France and the United Kingdom's move to more nuclear cooperation in response, and anxiety about China's intentions have all been game-changers. President Trump's pursuit of a continental "Golden Dome" missile defence system, while just as fanciful as President Reagan's "Star Wars" dream, has made its own contribution to ensuring that those potentially on the receiving end of US strikes want more, not fewer, nuclear weapons, to retain some serious retaliatory capability.

The hope that the nuclear ban treaty – the TPNW – would make a difference has proved illusory, partly because of its fairly obvious weaknesses. Drafted and negotiated more speedily than other arms control treaties of any significance, its aspirations were manifestly normative rather than practical, giving little confidence to countries abandoning their nuclear weapons that others would not take advantage of them.

It has three main problems, as seen by the nuclear-armed states. It is inattentive to the crucial question of verification, left to be addressed by an international authority to be designated by member states. (That said, progress on warhead dismantlement verification has been made by Norway- and UK-led research.) It is silent on the more crucial question of enforcement, understandable given that no one has a credible solution to the issue of how to respond to a rogue state breakout in a nuclear-weapon-free world. And the provision that nuclear-armed states joining the treaty submit to a time-bound schedule for the complete and irreversible elimination of their stockpiles has not been accepted by states nervous about going to zero while others still have nuclear weapons.

"Global zero" will remain for the foreseeable future an unattainable dream

All this is not to say that the TPNW has been either a waste of time or counterproductive. The idea of the ban treaty and the humanitarian consequences movement from which it was born has generated normative momentum. Global stigmatisation, delegitimisation and the will to prohibit nuclear weapons may not be sufficient for their elimination, but they are necessary conditions, and it is important that the effort be maintained.

The lesson that must be confronted is that "global zero" will remain for the foreseeable future an unattainable dream. But the arguments about the illusory rewards and obvious risks of nuclear weapons will remain indispensable in making the case for non-proliferation and risk reduction. These may be less ambitious nuclear arms control objectives, but in public policy one should never make the best the enemy of the merely good.

The challenge of non-proliferation

The Non-Proliferation Treaty (NPT), in force since 1970, has been remarkably successful in defying President Kennedy's prediction in 1963 that as many as twenty-five states would possess nuclear weapons by the end of the 1970s. But it is as fragile as it has ever been. Consensus – in particular about measures to further strengthen the safeguards regime at its heart – is proving ever more elusive: for the next five-yearly Review Conference, due in 2026, the NPT Preparatory Committee sessions have been unable to reach agreement on any recommendations, and the prospects for a substantive final outcome document are dismal. India, Pakistan and Israel remain outside the NPT, and North Korea walked away from it in 2003. Fears of further breakout are increasing in North-East Asia and Europe due to the loss of confidence in Trump's America, and in the Middle East due to the prospect of Iran responding to the humiliation of the assaults by Israel and the US by rushing to a bomb of its own.

The basic dynamic undermining the NPT has long been the unwillingness of its nuclear weapon states – and many of those supporting them (including Australia, at least under non-Labor governments) – to acknowledge that they have any serious obligation under Article VI of the treaty to take serious steps towards disarmament, notwithstanding that this was part of the bargain that the non-weapon states entered into in forgoing nuclear ambitions of their own.

The double-standards argument has acquired new resonance with the breathtaking hypocrisy involved in Israel – a state which never signed on to the NPT, and maintained a posture of "nuclear opacity" which enabled the US and others in the West to turn a blind eye to its development of a nuclear arsenal – launching, manifestly in breach of international law, a military attack on Iran, an NPT member with a problematic nuclear program, but one which no serious intelligence reports found had ever decided to weaponise, let alone use to mount an existential attack on the Jewish state.

Moreover, the US under Trump did its credibility no favours, not only by tearing up in 2018 the Joint Comprehensive Plan of Action (JCPOA) of 2015 – a triumph of cooperative diplomacy by all the major powers, including Russia and China, which had effectively quashed fears of any Iranian breakout for the next fifteen years – but also in responding to this year's tensions. Once Israel's opening barrage gave

Trump the sense that the door was open, he abandoned his previously stated preference for a diplomatic solution and, despite negotiations being active, opted for a quick military victory in which his insatiable presidential ego could bask.

At the time of this writing, in July 2025, the jury is still out as to what Iran's response will be. For all the damage that American bombs have done, and for all the difficulties of mounting a new clandestine program under US and Israeli intelligence eyes, Iran almost certainly retains a significant stockpile of enriched uranium, centrifuge capability and bomb-making know-how – as well as a fierce sense of national pride, shared by its population, however much the majority may despise the clerical regime. All of which could result in Iran being nuclear-armed within the next two or three years.

As head of the International Crisis Group in the early 2000s, I was heavily engaged in backchannel discussions in Tehran and elsewhere developing the "delayed limited enrichment" concept, which ultimately became central to the JCPOA. I was convinced then – and remain so today – that Ayatollah Khamenei's reluctance to approve nuclear weaponisation, as distinct from demonstrating a capacity to do so, was both rationally and religiously founded. But the actions of the US and Israel undercut the moderates and emboldened the hardliners. With Iran's head to the gun, it is possible that a JCPOA-Mark II can be negotiated – for example, with even tighter restrictions on enrichment, more intrusive inspections and an open-ended timeline. But nobody believes that will be easy.

If Iran goes nuclear, there is every prospect that the global non-proliferation dam will finally burst. In the Middle East, Saudi Arabia has vowed to follow suit, with Egypt and nearby Turkey also possibly joining an NPT exodus. In Europe, Germany and Poland have openly toyed with building nuclear weapons, not just relying on the UK and France to deter Russia if the US goes missing. In North-East Asia, the election of a more moderate government in Seoul has reduced concern about imminent nuclear breakout to counter perceived threats from North Korea and China, but public sentiment remains in favour (as it has been, at between 55 per cent and 75 per cent, for over a decade) of acquiring a capability. If that happens, pressure for Japan to follow suit may become irresistible, notwithstanding its history and very reluctant public.

If Iran goes nuclear, there is every prospect that the global non-proliferation dam will finally burst

What might fix these potential cracks in the NPT dam wall? Its more fissiparous parties becoming less ideologically purist and accepting the criticality of non-proliferation even if the weapons states remain insufferably hypocritical? All interested countries to use more effectively forums such as the UN and the G20 to put pressure on wavering states? "Rule-of-law supportive" states working harder on collaboration to similar effect? Maybe. But so long as the nuclear-armed states remain not only obdurately opposed to outright disarmament but resistant even to lesser arms control measures, such aspirations seem founded more in hope than in realistic expectation.

The challenge of risk reduction

In an environment where the achievement of global zero remains out of reach, it makes sense for those advocating for a nuclear-weapon-free world to focus on risk reduction, as many are now doing. The object would be to find common ground with policymakers who still see nuclear weapons as an ultimate deterrent and security guarantor but understand the risks involved and want to minimise them.

The most commonly proposed risk-reduction measures – and central elements in the "minimization" agenda proposed by the Australia–Japan International Commission on Nuclear Non-proliferation and Disarmament (ICNND) in 2009 – may be described as the "4 Ds". They are *Doctrine* (getting universal buy-in for a "No First Use" [NFU] commitment), *Deployment* (drastically reducing the number of weapons ready for immediate use), *De-alerting* (taking weapons off high-alert, launch-on-warning readiness) and *Decreased* numbers (dramatically reducing the global stockpile).

In many ways the most game-changing of these measures would be the universal embrace of No First Use, meaning that each nuclear-armed state would make an explicit declaration that it will not use nuclear weapons either preventively or pre-emptively against an adversary, nuclear-armed or not, and keeps them only for use or threat of use as retaliation following a nuclear strike against itself or its allies. A less robust formulation of essentially the same idea is a declaration that "the sole purpose of the possession of nuclear weapons is to deter the use of such weapons against one's own state and that of one's allies", which was the formula embraced by President Obama, and supported by President Biden, until both were dissuaded by noisy opposition from some NATO and Asia-Pacific allies keen to preserve a first-use option.

Only China and India currently claim to be committed to NFU. Russia abandoned an earlier pledge in the 1990s; France has long maintained a first-use posture; the United Kingdom, Pakistan and North Korea have not ruled it out; and Israel, as ever, refuses to confirm that it has nuclear weapons. But there continues to be widespread support for it among advocates for nuclear sanity, and for good reasons. These include that retaining a first-use option is dangerous, because it runs the risk of an adversary misreading its intentions and, fearing decapitation, launching a pre-emptive strike, precipitating an avoidable nuclear war. And that it is unnecessary, because the major nuclear powers all have immense conventional firepower, amply sufficient to deter or respond to chemical, biological or other non-nuclear attack.

The objection that NFU declarations are not believable with any state able to reverse in an instant any such commitment would be less strong if they were accompanied by measures like the three other "Ds" listed above. But even in their absence, it is important to acknowledge the extent to which military leaders do, in practice, pay close attention to others' declaratory policies, and the way in which these signals of intent shape the expectations of allies and adversaries alike, in what can either be a virtuous or vicious cycle.

All that said, too many of the nuclear-armed states show no willingness to come back to the arms control table, despite multiple calls for them to do so in UN and other multilateral forums, including at this year's Shangri-La defence summit in Singapore. The US is keen to negotiate an extension to New START, limiting the deployment of strategic weapons, but Russia is dragging its feet. China has the capacity to play a leadership role, given the credibility it has acquired over many years for its "minimal deterrence" posture and general restraint on nuclear issues, if not for its transparency. But it has been reluctant to do so while the size of its nuclear arsenal remains so much smaller than those of the US and Russia.

When it comes to nuclear risk reduction, the most crucial immediate need, as strategists such as Lawrence Freedman have pointed out, is to restore between the key players the dialogue – and the trust and confidence that flows from such contact – that has been the central value of past arms control measures. Even the most bitter antagonists have a shared interest in avoiding nuclear confrontation. It is important – not least at times of crisis – that senior officers and officials know each other and understand each other's concerns, and have easy and open lines of communication. On this front, unhappily, around the world, we are currently a long way from where we need to be.

Australia's role

On big global issues there is only so much change that can, realistically, be accomplished by even the most creative and energetic of middle powers, as Australia has periodically been over the decades. Any influence that we wield has to rely on diplomatic persuasion and coalition-building, not on the exercise of raw military or economic might. But we have made significant contributions in the past to nuclear arms control, as well as on other weapons of mass destruction issues, in particular bringing to a conclusion the Chemical Weapons Convention in 1993. And we can again, even in an environment as dispiriting as the one we now confront.

The commitment of successive Australian governments to the NPT ... has always been clear and unequivocal

Our past achievements include the Keating government's initiation in 1996 of the Canberra Commission, the first international blue-ribbon panel – including political, economic, military and environmental leaders and experts from around the world – to argue effectively for global zero, and much quoted in international debate since; our lead advocacy role in the ICJ Advisory Opinions Case in 1996; the crucial role played by Ambassador Richard Butler in securing in 1995 (under the Labor government) the permanent extension of the NPT, and in 1996 (under the Coalition government) the adoption of the CTBT; the initiation by the Rudd government in 2007 of the joint Australia–Japan ICNND, which not only made a strong case for an ultimate elimination agenda but mapped a realistic step-by-step risk-reduction path to get there; and the co-founding in 2010 of the cross-regional Non-Proliferation and Disarmament Initiative (NPDI) to take forward consensus outcomes of the NPT Review Conference.

We have also been among the global leaders in developing, through the IAEA and other mechanisms, effective safeguards, nuclear security and test monitoring strategies, including concluding in 1997 the world's first IAEA safeguards Additional Protocol. This has been recognised, inter alia, by the election in 2021 of Dr Robert Floyd to head the CTBT Organization (CTBTO). Labor governments have been generous in supporting academic and non-governmental organisation efforts to advance the nuclear arms control agenda, including the establishment of the Asia-Pacific Leadership Network nuclear advocacy organisation in 2011, and the Centre for Nuclear Non-Proliferation and Disarmament at the Australian National University. And it should be acknowledged, even if the Morrison government ungraciously declined to offer congratulations, that the 2017 Nobel Peace Prize winner, the International Campaign to Abolish Nuclear Weapons (ICAN), was founded in Australia.

When it comes to advancing the case for nuclear *disarmament*, probably the best we can do in the present environment is make supportive statements at ministerial and diplomatic level at the UN and elsewhere, spelling out – not looking anxiously over our shoulder at Washington – all the arguments summarised in this paper to the effect that whatever deterrent utility nuclear weapons may conceivably have had in the past, the risk of their continued possession by anyone, in today's fragile, multiplayer and increasingly cyber-driven nuclear world, far outweighs any benefit. If that means that we can no longer rely in a crisis on US extended *nuclear* deterrence (as distinct from extended *conventional* deterrence), that simply acknowledges what has always been the case: the US will never contemplate sacrificing Miami for Melbourne.

As to whether we should put our money where our mouth is when it comes to signing the TPNW, some of the concerns which have so far inhibited Australia from doing so have no substance. This treaty does not undermine the NPT, and its non-universality and technical weaknesses are not in themselves showstoppers: we could work from inside to rectify its problems and promote its wider acceptance. But the problem Australia does face is that the treaty quite specifically bans any form of assistance to nuclear-weapons-related activity, and this would make it impossible for us to continue to jointly host, in particular, the US early-warning, intelligence-gathering and targeting facility at Pine Gap, which would in turn be very much a showstopper for the alliance. While some would argue that is a consummation devoutly to be wished, it is rather a lot to bite off as the price of joining a treaty with no practical teeth.

When it comes to supporting nuclear *non-proliferation*, the commitment of successive Australian governments to the NPT – and to strengthening its regime in every way possible, including through universal adoption of the Additional Protocol on inspections – has always been clear and unequivocal, and that should obviously continue. As to whether the AUKUS nuclear fuel-propelled submarines project is at odds with that, whatever the force of the arguments (including deliverability, cost–benefit and impact on our sovereign agency) for ending this wholly misconceived project, its proliferation potential is not one of them: the new safeguards protocols being painfully negotiated at the IAEA should put at rest such concerns.

We should also maintain our commitment to CTBT/CTBTO implementation, the stalled Fissile Material Cut-off Treaty negotiation, and the kind of nuclear security measures recommended by the successive Obama-initiated Nuclear Security Summits. We should emphasise in all relevant forums our traditional support for nuclear-weapon-free zones, and lend our weight to the concept of a North-East Asia NWFZ embracing Japan, South Korea and North Korea (and perhaps also Mongolia), with accompanying guarantees from the US, China and Russia – hugely difficult as this will be to implement, recognising that the task for North Korea is no longer non-proliferation but disarmament.

What we should *not* do is respond to potential breakouts from the NPT with the illegal and irresponsible use of military force. If there is an Iranian nuclear threat, only cooperative diplomacy of the kind we saw in 2015 can end it, not US bombs.

When it comes to supporting nuclear *risk reduction*, our status as a close US ally and, as such, one of the "nuclear umbrella" states should give us a significant role. In the Trumpian world we now inhabit, where allies are at least as likely to be seen as encumbrances rather than assets, there may not be much room left for influence, but that should not stop us trying.

My highest priority would be to support the struggling but still growing international movement for the universal adoption of No First Use doctrine by the nuclear-armed states. It should not be a matter of pride for us that when both President Obama and President Biden were attracted to going down this path (or at least to its "sole purpose" functional equivalent), Australia was one of those nervous Asia-Pacific and East European allies who failed to support them. The failure to make progress then should not be seen as the end of the argument. One of the many peculiarities of the Trump administration is that the president seems to have a visceral distaste for nuclear weapons, and it may be that we would be pushing at an open door.

> **Being and being seen to be a good international citizen ... is a national interest in its own right**

One final initiative would be helpful: Prime Minister Albanese should make a major speech comprehensively drawing together the key threads of the nuclear arms control story – commitment to the goal of a nuclear-weapon-free world, to nuclear non-proliferation and to risk reduction – and explaining how Australia can, realistically, contribute to each objective. His government is not given to making big, visionary, conceptual statements but this would be a good opportunity to break out.

It has long been my belief that being and being seen to be a good international citizen – a decent country, committed to "purposes beyond ourselves", as Hedley Bull would put it – is a national interest in its own right, to be pursued not just as a moral imperative but for its soft power returns with the same commitment we show to the traditional duo of national interests in security and prosperity. There can be no more obvious way of demonstrating our decency than by making a clear declaration, at the highest political level, of our determination to contribute to ridding the world once and for all of the humanitarian horror, and existential risk to life on this planet as we know it, of nuclear war. ■

RED SUNRISE

China's rapid nuclear expansion

Rajeswari Pillai Rajagopalan

In the late 2010s, China began a dramatic expansion and modernisation of its nuclear forces – including rapidly constructing hundreds of underground missile launchers across the country. The US Department of Defense estimates that China could have 1000 nuclear warheads by the end of the 2020s – a significant shift from the roughly 300 warheads it has maintained for decades. Given the deafening silence from China about the logic and goal of this expansion, others in the region will likely make worst-case assumptions and plan to enhance their own military procurement programs, although among them only India is a nuclear power. China's nuclear expansion is likely to have destabilising regional consequences, including for Australia's security.

There are many unknowns and uncertainties around China's expansion of its nuclear arsenal. Is it planning to match the US and Russian numbers of long-range missiles? What would such an arsenal mean for the region? Will China continue focusing on intermediate-range ballistic missiles (IRBMs), which have ranges between 3000 and 5500 kilometres, for regional deterrence? Given that China already has mobile missile platforms, what is the purpose of its extensive construction of missile silos (long metal tubes placed vertically underground from which missiles are launched)? Is China also modernising its long-range bombers? Another critical question concerns China's nuclear doctrine: will it shift its targeting strategy? Until now, China is presumed to have been targeting cities, but the development of more accurate missiles indicates it will shift to targeting the nuclear forces of its adversaries. These questions only confirm the opacity of China's nuclear build-up and add to worries in the region.

China's nuclear expansion

For decades, China's nuclear force development was gradual and measured. From the 1970s, it developed a mix of both intercontinental ballistic missiles (ICBMs) and IRBMs, with IRBMs meant for use within the Indo-Pacific region against neighbours such as India and Japan. Unlike that of the United States or the Soviet Union/Russia, Chinese military technology has never been sophisticated enough to equip it with capable long-range bombers or submarine-launched missiles. Also, as China's military was traditionally a land-based force, its focus was on land-based systems even on the nuclear front. As a result, most of China's nuclear force relies on land-based missiles.

Since the 1980s, China has deployed several ICBMs, variants of the Dongfeng 5 (DF-5), with ranges of more than 10,000 kilometres, allowing it to hit distant targets such as Australia and the continental United States. Some of these were also fitted with multiple independently targetable re-entry vehicles (MIRVs) – which is another way of saying multiple warheads. Some missiles were equipped with up to five warheads. One downside of the DF-5, despite its long range, was that they were silo-based and liquid-fuelled, making them both vulnerable to attack and slow to launch during a crisis.

Responding to these limitations, China began shifting to solid-fuelled and road-mobile systems. This included new ICBMs such as the Dongfeng 31 (DF-31), which has a range of around 7000 kilometres and deployed in 2006, and the Dongfeng 41 (DF-41), which has a range of 12,000 kilometres and deployed in 2019. These missiles are road-mobile and rail-mobile, making them difficult to detect and target. China's new Dongfeng 21 (DF-21) IRBMs have begun to replace the older Dongfeng 4 (DF-4) missiles. The DF-21s can carry both nuclear and conventional warheads, making the risk of discrimination – deciding whether an incoming missile is carrying a nuclear or a conventional warhead – a significant challenge for adversaries. The DF-21s are now being slowly replaced with the Dongfeng 26 (DF-26), which is solid-fuelled and road-mobile.

The Chinese nuclear expansion primarily involves warheads and long-range missiles

On the naval front, too, China has been making important strides, enhancing its nuclear triad. China's naval leg includes six Type 094 Jin-class nuclear-powered ballistic missile submarines (SSBNs), each armed with JL-2 submarine-launched ballistic missiles (SLBMs). These SLBMs are derivatives from the land-based DF-31, with an estimated range of 7000 kilometres. However, many experts believe that China's SSBNs are still "rudimentary". Whether these submarines go on routine long-duration deterrent patrols is not certain. If they cannot, their strategic utility is limited. But China is making impressive progress in this area: it is believed to be equipping the Jin-class SSBNs with newer missiles, the JL-3 SLBM, which has a longer range of around 12,000 kilometres and can carry multiple warheads. China is also planning to introduce the next-generation Type 096 Tang-class SSBNs in the near future. These newer missile submarines are quieter and technologically more advanced, and are thus considered more viable for long-duration strategic patrols. The new platform will qualitatively improve China's sea-based nuclear force.

The air leg of China's nuclear triad is generally considered its weakest. The only bomber aircraft currently in operation is the Xi'an H-6, which is a twin-engine, subsonic, long-range aircraft from the 1960s. As an old bomber with limited capabilities, the H-6 is not a big threat to anyone – unless it's armed with long-range stand-off missiles. For example, it can carry the CJ-10 cruise missile, which has a range of 1500 kilometres and can be armed with a nuclear warhead. But China is reported to be working on a new long-range stealth bomber, the Xi'an H-20, thought to be comparable to the US Northrop B-2 Spirit stealth bomber. The H-20 is supposed to have a range of more than 8000 kilometres, with a payload capacity of over 10 tonnes. It is still under development and untested, and possibly a decade away from operational deployment.

The Chinese nuclear expansion primarily involves warheads and long-range missiles, especially those in silos. Matt Korda and Hans Kristensen of the Federation of American Scientists (FAS) have stated that China is constructing at least three large missile silo fields near Yumen, Hami and Ordos, in north-central China. Satellite imagery supports these claims, as do longstanding US assessments that China aims to at least double its nuclear warhead stockpile within the next decade. FAS reports that China has made substantial progress at these silo sites, as well as at a People's Liberation Army Rocket Force training facility near Jilantai, Inner Mongolia. China has not officially acknowledged or denied these developments. According to available data, the Yumen site, first revealed by the Middlebury Institute in June, includes approximately 120 silos. The Hami site, identified by FAS in July, has around 110 silos, while the Ordos location, revealed by a US Air University research unit, features about forty. Each of these fields reportedly includes support infrastructure such as launch-control centres and base facilities.

Until recently, China's nuclear stockpile was estimated to be around 300 warheads, but it is now steadily growing. FAS, which has monitored this increase, notes that in 2019 China had about 290 nuclear warheads, for delivery by 180–190 land-based ballistic missiles, and forty-eight sea-based missiles and bombers. The US Defense Intelligence Agency (DIA) supported this estimate, describing China's arsenal as in the "low couple hundreds". In its 2020 report, FAS revised its estimate to around 350 warheads, including roughly 272 deployed on over 240 operational land-based missiles, forty-eight on SLBMs, and twenty nuclear gravity bombs for bombers. The remaining seventy-eight warheads were believed to be designated for missiles not yet deployed. The 2020 report projected further growth in China's stockpile, although it remained significantly smaller than those of the United States and Russia, which have over 5000 warheads each. The most recent *Bulletin of the Atomic Scientists* assessment on China's nuclear weapons, made in 2025, suggests that the number of China's warheads has climbed to more than 400. Expectations are that China will expand its arsenal to over 1000 warheads by the 2030s.

Why the expansion?

Understanding why China is engaging in this expansion will inform how countries such as Australia respond. Is it routine or does it portend something dire?

Since China has provided no explanation for this massive and sudden expansion, it is up to other governments and experts to make sense of what is driving it. One obvious possibility is that it is simply a function of China's growing wealth: it can now afford a much larger and more capable military, including an expanded nuclear force. After all, China's conventional military forces have also been expanding and acquiring new equipment. On the other hand, the nuclear expansion appears to be on a different trajectory to the conventional military modernisation, and it started much later. If the growth were simply the result of bigger budgetary allocation, the nuclear expansion should have started at least a decade earlier, when conventional modernisation took off.

Another possible explanation is a change in the political calculus. For a long time China maintained that it did not have to compete in the nuclear domain to be a great power, and that a conventionally strong military was evidence of its great-power status. But China under Xi has a different idea of what a great power looks like. For Xi, China must achieve parity with the United States and other major powers in every matrix, including in the nuclear domain. Internal signals in China suggest that enhanced nuclear capabilities may be part of the vision Xi articulated at the 20th Party Congress in October 2022. His vision encompassed the establishment of "a strong system of strategic deterrence", including expanded "new domain forces" with advanced combat capabilities, fast-tracked development of unmanned and intelligent platforms, and stronger integration of information networks for military operations. Strategic deterrence was not part of Xi's 2017 Party Congress speech, but he emphasised its importance in the Fourteenth Five-Year Plan

China, like India, views nuclear weapons as political tools, intended for deterrence

(2021–25), highlighting goals such as ensuring "high-calibre strategic deterrence and joint operation systems". If Xi's vision is indeed the reason for China's nuclear weapons expansion, then China is unlikely to stop at 1000 warheads, as the United States expects. It may keep going until it has at least as many as the Americans and the Russians.

Another possibility is that China is responding to US missile defence efforts, building more weapons to ensure that at least some could get through any possible US missile shield. But there have been no technological breakthroughs in missile defences, nor was there any US plan for a national missile defence shield when China started its nuclear expansion about a decade ago.

Kristensen and Korda suggest that China's motivations may go beyond concerns about the United States, and could be driven by competition with Russia and India. While the India–China competition is direct and straightforward, Beijing's relationship with Moscow is more complicated. They have moved periodically from allies to adversaries and back. In the early Cold War, the Soviet Union and China were partners against the United States, but in the 1970s China partnered with America against the Soviets. After the Cold War, China and Russia have become increasingly close in jointly siding against the United States.

Beijing's nuclear doctrine

Countries such as Australia must also assess whether China's expanding nuclear force presages any change in how it might use its nuclear weapons. China's nuclear policy for several decades had a limited objective of deterring what it called "nuclear blackmail" by the United States and the Soviet Union. This meant China took a restrained approach to how it developed its nuclear force. In fact, Mao Zedong was famous for his remark that "six are enough". China maintained a small arsenal for several decades, along with a commitment to a minimum deterrent strategy and a "No First Use" (NFU) doctrine. China, like India, views nuclear weapons as political tools, intended for deterrence and not as warfighting weapons. The limited size of the arsenal inspired reasonable confidence in China's NFU policy among its neighbours. So what does a larger force mean for Beijing's nuclear doctrine?

While an expanded nuclear arsenal may not be in line with an NFU policy, there is nothing, at least in the public domain, that suggests China is giving up on its posture. In terms of nuclear doctrine, therefore, it appears China still adheres to its NFU policy and to the concept of a minimum deterrent. Yet China's sudden and rapid nuclear expansion suggests it may be rethinking its approach to nuclear weapons. Can a force of over 1000 warheads be compatible with "minimum" deterrence?

There have been internal debates on this within China. Following Russia's invasion of Ukraine in February 2022 and its subsequent nuclear sabre-rattling, some Chinese voices questioned the NFU policy. A Japanese media report, sourcing a study by China's National Defense University, called for a review of the NFU policy, particularly to deter US intervention in a potential conflict over Taiwan. According to these reports, the recommendations and debate were considered by the PRC's Central Military Commission (CMC), but there was no change to China's official NFU policy.

China's formal doctrinal position allows it to project an image of itself as a responsible nuclear stakeholder with moral superiority above the United States, which does not have an NFU policy. In a Chinese Ministry of Foreign Affairs statement issued on 23 July 2024, China reiterated its NFU policy, saying that "nuclear weapons cannot be used and nuclear war must not be fought", and that "China's development of nuclear weapons is not for the purpose of threatening other countries, but for self-defense, safeguarding national strategic security, and contributing to world peace and stability". However, China could develop riskier policies within its existing NFU doctrine. It could, for instance, engage in non-nuclear attacks on the adversary's command and control system. Its "launch on warning" posture, its use of nuclear capable dual-use systems, and its introduction of artificial intelligence (AI) into its early-warning and targeting systems and even command and control systems can all be risky and destabilising.

While China may not give up its NFU policy despite its weapons expansion, new questions have emerged about how and whether its NFU stance applies to territories that it considers its own. For instance, how would China's NFU policy work in India–China border areas, or in an Indian province such as Arunachal Pradesh, which China claims? Would this ambiguity restrain India in a conventional border conflict? China is keeping its adversaries guessing as to how it would respond in a conventional conflict, and so is forcing them to submit to it even without making nuclear threats.

Similarly, China has brought complexities to its NFU posture by allowing for flexibility within its existing nuclear doctrine. China is believed to be readying a "launch under attack" posture. This would mean it could launch its weapons if it were certain that enemy missiles were headed in its direction.

China could develop riskier policies within its existing NFU doctrine

China is also developing a "launch on warning" posture within its existing NFU stance. This would permit it to attack another country based on intelligence and surveillance reports that suggested an imminent attack by that country. China is also thought to be putting in place elements of a first-strike policy, should it run into problems with conventional military operations.

China has been making significant investment in space-based sensors and early-warning systems, so its possible adoption of "launch on warning" and "launch under attack" postures comes as no surprise. Russia and China have also been collaborating on early-warning systems for the last five or six years. Media reports in 2020 said that the Russian-Chinese missile attack early-warning system was close to completion, and that it would rely on data from Russian Tundra satellites and Voronezh modular ground-based radar stations within Chinese territory. The Chinese push for a "launch on warning" posture indicates its confidence in the Russian early-warning systems. But China will want to continue with its ambiguity and some hazy red lines so that its adversaries will remain unsure.

China's NFU policy, like all NFU policies, is merely declaratory. There is nothing that legally binds China to this stance. It should therefore be seen more as a rhetorical position that can be altered, should China find itself in a weak position. More importantly, as China expands its nuclear force, it might seek a doctrinal shift to mirror those of the US and Russia.

China is learning a great deal from the Russian invasion of Ukraine. Beijing has carefully analysed how Russia's nuclear deterrence prevented the US and NATO from becoming actively involved in the defence of Ukraine. President Putin's threats to use tactical nuclear weapons had a significant impact on decision-makers in Brussels and Washington. President Xi, who is categorical about unifying Taiwan with the mainland with or without force, may hope to prevent the United States and its allies from getting involved in a conflict over Taiwan in the same way.

Australia's options

China's nuclear expansion has obvious implications for the strategic balance in the Indo-Pacific. While Australia is not a nuclear weapons state, it is an ally of the United States and depends on US extended deterrence for protection from nuclear threats. Australia also has investments in major nuclear-powered capability arrangements such as AUKUS, which will eventually provide it with nuclear-powered (but not nuclear-armed) submarines. The establishment of AUKUS was driven more by China's general aggression in the region than by its nuclear expansion, but the latter has only intensified Australian security concerns.

Australia has not actively contemplated developing its own nuclear deterrent in decades, but a new debate has now begun, driven by China's military and nuclear expansion. Another motivating factor are concerns about whether the United States under President Trump can be depended on to protect Australia with its extended deterrence.

For decades, Australia has recognised that it could not secure itself against a nuclear-armed great-power adversary. The promise that the American nuclear arsenal would protect it is no longer a certainty, as domestic political and economic changes in the United States prompt its leaders to question whether it benefits from such international commitments. While it still seems inconceivable that the United States would withdraw from its commitments to its allies entirely – the United States receives economic and security gains from them, after all – the current American debate about its global strategy raises uncomfortable questions for its allies – and especially for a country such as Australia, which is relatively weak and is proximate to the rising great power that is China.

China's strengthened deterrence measures could restrain Australia's ability to respond even in a conventional confrontation. For example, if Australia were contemplating responding to a crisis in the

South China Sea or in Taiwan, it might fear nuclear escalation by China. Similarly, India has for decades been constrained in its responses to Pakistan-supported terrorism because of fear of nuclear escalation.

China's nuclear expansion/modernisation has contributed to an escalating arms race in the region and beyond. China's nuclear force could have a direct bearing on India's nuclear arsenal and posture, and China's drive to achieve nuclear parity with the United States and Russia could push others in the region, such as Japan and South Korea, to serious consideration of nuclear options; public support for this is growing in both those countries. Even if Australia does not go down the path of nuclear weapons, it will feel pressure to raise its overall deterrence game by other means – such as long-range strike capabilities, missile defence systems, and cyber and space defensive and offensive capability developments – all of which can create an atmosphere of instability. A general climate of proliferation, in which various countries decide that they would be better off having their own deterrence capability, will impact Australian security and the stability of the region. Australia as well as other countries in the region need to carefully monitor Chinese behaviour that could be risky and destabilising in the broader regional context. For example, China's expanding arsenal, including long-range, nuclear-capable, dual-use missiles, could raise the risk of nuclear escalation.

We need to consider also the effects of China's nuclear expansion on arms control. There has been little progress in arms control in decades, and existing measures are eroding in various areas, including nuclear proliferation and outer-space management. The United States has been calling for China to join it and Russia in nuclear arms control talks, but China has resisted until now, with the excuse that its force was so much smaller. Its nuclear expansion creates an opportunity for Washington to more forcefully call on Beijing to join these arms control discussions.

Adding one more actor would complicate negotiations, especially if the Americans feel the Russians and Chinese are ganging up against them, but China's participation could reduce Russia's importance in global affairs, as it would no longer be the sole power with the special status of parity with the United States. Indeed, Russia would become the poor cousin, as both the Americans and the Chinese would be much richer than and technologically superior to the Russians. This dynamic could cause additional complications, perhaps making Russia even more intransigent, which is certainly not something Australia wants.

Australia must consider the effect of China's nuclear expansion on Beijing's strategic behaviour

Finally, Australia must consider the effect of China's nuclear expansion on Beijing's strategic behaviour. Would a China with 1500 or 2000 nuclear warheads become not only more difficult to deter but also more aggressive and assertive? Would such a China create conditions that lead to general instability in the region? National leaders, when engaging in risky behaviour, frequently miscalculate both their own chances of success and the resolve of others. The assumption so far has been that nuclear weapons would induce some caution because of the consequences of nuclear escalation. Seven decades of experience with nuclear crises suggests that this notion has some validity – but it is also true that we have repeatedly been engaged in nuclear crises.

China's nuclear expansion is unnecessary and potentially dangerous. But it is unlikely that Canberra or anyone else will be able to convince Beijing to moderate its behaviour. Australian leaders, as well as leaders in the region, need to consider the consequences of China's behaviour and set clear markers about acceptable and unacceptable behaviour. This will not be easy, but the alternatives are even more unpalatable. ■

THE FIX *Solving Australia's foreign affairs challenges*

Gordon Noble & Nick Wood on How Australia Should Facilitate Climate Investment in the Indo-Pacific

"Australia [is] well-placed to support our region to build climate resilience while also enabling economies to grow in a sustainable way ... It is clearly in Australia's economic and strategic interests to assist its neighbours to mitigate the potential worst outcomes of climate change."

THE PROBLEM: The impacts of climate change are upon us. The mounting evidence of extreme weather events, exemplified by the regular breaking of climatic records, demonstrates what scientists have long been predicting. Without rapid decarbonisation of the world's economy, we can expect average global surface air temperatures to exceed 2 degrees Celsius of warming above pre-industrial levels before 2050. Climate change is already driving geopolitical risk via increased local vulnerability, worsening health outcomes, forced migration and social instability.

The United States' decision to walk away from its Paris Agreement commitments risks slowing efforts to decarbonise national economies, which could push global temperatures beyond 2.5 degrees Celsius. We are already in what the Network for Greening the Financial System, a group that includes 145 central banks and financial institutions, calls a "fragmented world" scenario. According to this assessment, delayed and divergent climate policy ambition globally is leading to a greater chance of events such as heatwaves, flooding and drought, and is adding to the costs of measures to reduce emissions, such as carbon price mechanisms and renewable energy developments.

Analysis conducted in 2021 by Chatham House for the UK government concluded that climate change will "drive political instability and greater national insecurity, and fuel regional and international conflict". The impact for our region is profound, with the Pacific Islands Forum declaring in 2018 that "climate change remains the single greatest threat to the livelihoods, security and wellbeing of the peoples of the Pacific".

The United Nations has stated that unprecedented levels of capital flows, in the order of trillions of US dollars each year, are required to transition to a zero-carbon economy and to develop sufficient resilience to the physical impacts of climate change. The 2023 edition of the UN Environment Programme's *Adaptation Gap Report* estimated that the annual funding shortfall in developing countries alone is between US$194 billion and US$366 billion, some fifteen times more than the current finance flows.

One of the main reasons for this gap is that many developing countries have a lack of climate financial capability. Our region has few mature financial markets, such as stock exchanges, through which climate-aligned capital can flow. Insufficient country-specific climate data and data on risk and vulnerability adds to the challenges for investors.

The consequences of a lack of climate financial capability can be observed in well-intentioned but scientifically naive "green" investments, such as the development of transmission lines in locations that may be impacted by future wildfires. A key question is how climate financial capability can be developed and enhanced in the Indo-Pacific.

THE PROPOSAL: The Australian government should establish a partnership between Treasury, the Department of Foreign Affairs and Trade, the Commonwealth Scientific and Industrial Research Organisation (CSIRO), the Department of Defence, and Australian universities and financial institutions to support climate financial capacity across regional economies. An opportunity exists to establish the partnership as an output of the UN Conference of the Parties (COP 31) in 2026. This would demonstrate Australia's commitment to taking coordinated action in climate policy.

The current approach is dominated by large, multilateral development banks such as the World Bank and the Asian Development Bank, which act too slowly to mitigate the impacts of climate change. These banks have a strong preference for large-scale "nation-building projects" and a relative lack of expertise in community-level resilience projects. The proposed Australian partnership would facilitate investment in companies in the region that provide climate solutions on the ground.

The partnership would focus on supporting the development of regional stock exchanges to enable the flow of climate capital. The amount of capital that flows into a stock exchange is a measure of its potential to finance sustainable development. Some parts of the world, including in the Indo-Pacific, are subject to "droughts of capital" that lead to a loss of resilience and increase the likelihood of systemic crises. The partnership could support businesses on regional stock exchanges to use climate data to make informed decisions, while also engaging with large pools of capital to drive investment.

WHY IT WILL WORK: Australia has three qualities that make it well-placed to support our region to build climate resilience while enabling economies to grow in a sustainable way.

First, Australia has a world-class capability in climate science across the CSIRO, the Bureau of Meteorology and the university sector. Australia is the only nation in the Southern Hemisphere that can build, sustain and run earth system models, the highly complex computer programs that integrate the interactions of atmosphere, ocean, land, ice and the biosphere. These are the fundamental tools of climate risk analysis.

Second, Australia has a sophisticated financial sector. Our superannuation funds have accumulated $4 trillion in capital, which they are actively seeking to invest overseas.

Finally, Australia's civil engineering sector has expertise in building infrastructure in challenging (and changing) environments. Our civil engineering expertise could support the region to develop critical infrastructure, such as local renewable energy micro-grids, electric vehicle charging networks in dense urban areas, waste management and recycling plants, and city-wide flood resilience systems.

It is clearly in Australia's economic and strategic interests to assist its neighbours to mitigate the potential worst outcomes of climate change. The alternative would be truly terrifying. For example, the large-scale failure of water and power supplies in an Asian megacity during the type of extreme heatwave projected to occur by the 2050s would lead to a level of population mortality unprecedented in the modern human era.

The success of any political action depends on timing, and for Australia – which has a duty to bring a new and pragmatic proposal to COP 31 that will assist our Pacific and Asian neighbours to manage climate risks – the timing for a partnership on climate finance capability is just about perfect. ■

Reviews

The Big Fix: Rebuilding Australia's National Security
Albert Palazzo
Melbourne University Press

Albert Palazzo's new book is a timely addition to the national debate on defence strategy. It arrives in the midst of growing strategic uncertainty, as discussions about the future of the US–Australia alliance, defence spending, Australia's nuclear-powered submarine pathway, emerging technologies, and lessons from recent conflicts in Ukraine and the Red Sea shape Australia's defence landscape.

In *The Big Fix: Rebuilding Australia's National Security*, Palazzo, a career academic and accomplished author, critiques Australia's defence policy, arguing that its alignment with the United States, its neglect of climate-related security risks and its preoccupation with China mean that reassessment is urgently needed. He proposes a shift to a more self-reliant defence philosophy, which he calls the "strategic defensive".

To support this shift, Palazzo begins by targeting a centrepiece of Australia's current defence agenda, AUKUS, which he sees as evidence of Australia's "sub-imperial" status. He argues that nuclear-powered submarines may become obsolete due to advances in detection technologies, reviving the old trope of "transparent oceans" – a claim that rings hollow to anyone who has tried to find submarines at sea. Palazzo also claims that Australia's overarching strategic documents – the 2023 Defence Strategic Review and the 2024 National Defence Strategy – place disproportionate focus on the China threat, overlooking other challenges, particularly the security impacts of climate change.

While Palazzo is right to highlight the importance of emerging challenges such as climate change, his critique of Australia's defence posture conflates national security and defence strategy. A national security strategy directs all elements of national power towards a set of security objectives, while a defence strategy directs the military aspects of national power. The National Defence Strategy is not responsible for climate policy. While climate change might contribute to regional instability that could eventually require military involvement, even peacekeeping in a deteriorating region, as Palazzo asserts, this is not the current reality. Presently, the region isn't facing conflict driven by climate change, but it is experiencing daily the impact of China's growing military aggression. It is therefore difficult to accept Palazzo's argument that climate change should be the primary focus of Australia's National Defence Strategy.

Similarly, Palazzo views the China threat through the lens of Australia's "sub-imperial" relationship with the United States. He characterises China as an Asian hegemon and regional tensions as a function of great-power competition. In doing so, he downplays China's demonstrated aggression around Taiwan and in the South China Sea, behaviour that directly undermines the interests of Australia, which depends heavily on the maritime domain for its security and prosperity.

Palazzo's emphasis on the low likelihood of a Chinese invasion of Australia overlooks the fact that Australia's interests extend far beyond its territory. Australia relies on maritime trade and undersea internet cables to keep its economy – and any future war effort – functioning. You do not need to attack Australia in order to coerce Australia; Palazzo's misunderstanding of this underpins his broader defence recommendations.

Drawing on a brief history of military thinking at the strategic and tactical levels, Palazzo roots his concept of the "strategic defensive" in Australia's desire to remain a status quo power. Although *The Big Fix* does not clearly define the strategic defensive, Palazzo argues that Australia is naturally suited to a defensive posture due to its status quo orientation, its relatively modest military power and its geography. He contends that, with the right modern weapons, Australia could impose enough cost on an aggressor from its own territory to deter attack. Under this philosophy, Palazzo suggests, Australia's aim in war would be to make conflict so costly that the adversary agrees to return to the pre-war status quo.

In many ways, Palazzo's strategic defensive echoes the 2024 National Defence Strategy's concept of "deterrence by denial". However, he is quick to argue that "perhaps the most dangerous element" of the National Defence Strategy is its emphasis on deterrence. He describes deterrence as a "problematic" strategy, reliant on a nation's ability to impose unacceptable costs and to communicate that threat credibly. While he is right to highlight the challenges of deterrence, the more pressing issue is that Australia's unclassified defence strategy lacks clarity about what is being deterred, at whom it is aimed and how it will be achieved. All are critical elements of an effective deterrence strategy.

While Palazzo argues for replacing Australia's "deterrence by denial" strategy with a "strategic defensive" philosophy, his formulation of the strategic defensive is equally problematic. His concept is clearly threat-driven. He writes that "the first step in the provision of security is to understand the threats the state may face". Yet effective strategy begins not with threats but with understanding a state's vital interests – what it is that must be protected – before considering how those interests might be threatened. Australia's vital interests include access to maritime trade and undersea communication cables, and regional stability.

Not having assessed these vital interests, Palazzo's development of the strategic defensive leads him to frame Australia's power-projection capabilities, including nuclear-powered submarines, as merely supporting what he describes as the United States' strategy of the "strategic offensive". He underestimates the central role of the maritime domain in Australia's security and the need for power projection to defend maritime vulnerabilities, such as trade dependency, and to address threats at range. Australia's geographical distance is only a benefit if we make the most of it. Combating threats at range gives Australia a much greater change of defeating them. In doing so, he adopts a dated, land-centric view of Australian strategy – a common pitfall for academic theorists. This oversight leads to the most significant concern with Palazzo's thesis: the capability recommendations he proposes to support his strategy.

While Palazzo concedes that his capability recommendations are not extensive, those he does propose to support the strategic defensive appear poorly considered. He focuses on a few specific changes – notably, the immediate cancellation of all crewed naval platforms in favour of yet-to-be-developed autonomous systems, the acquisition of a large fleet of transport aircraft from which to launch long-range missiles, and greater investment in Army firepower. Although this summary simplifies his argument, the focus on territorial long-range strike closely mirrors Sam Roggeveen's "echidna strategy" and carries similar flaws. It leaves exposed Australia's seaborne supply lines and critical dependencies such as fuel, fertiliser and ammunition. Protecting Australia's maritime vulnerabilities and meeting threats at range requires the ability to project power, including expansive naval and air capabilities. Palazzo's recommendation to abandon all crewed ships and submarines contradicts this need. The autonomous systems he proposes do not yet exist – and even if they did, they could not fulfil such a broad range of functions.

The Big Fix challenges orthodoxy, but its central thesis and capability prescriptions lack practical grounding. Still, it prompts the kind of contestation Australia's defence policy debate needs.

Jennifer Parker

The Taiwan Story: How a Small Island Will Dictate the Global Future
Kerry Brown
Penguin

Australia thinks a lot about Taiwan, but almost never about the Taiwanese. For decades, Taiwan has been a metonym impelling Australia to define its foreign policy and international outlook as a dilemma. That dilemma is to reconcile Australia's alliance commitment to the United States, which has security assurances for Taiwan, with good relations with a rising China that threatens Taiwan's security.

Canberra uses arcane diplomatic language and has a "one China" policy that leaves its position on Taiwan's status ambiguous in order to quiesce the issue. But on the horizon is an imagined choice between the US and China in a "war over Taiwan". For some, the choice between an alliance with a capricious military superpower and the prosperity conferred by exporting to China is self-evident. For others, Taiwan validates a commitment to a US-led order and opposition to Beijing's Leninist authoritarian vision.

But Taiwan is also a real place with real people. The Taiwanese have their own complex history of imperialism, colonialism, authoritarianism and democracy. Understanding Taiwan, and the Taiwanese, is crucial to examining the assumptions that shape Australia's foreign policy debates and nation-building vision.

Kerry Brown's *The Taiwan Story: How a Small Island Will Dictate the Global Future* is timely, then, and arrives alongside the recent publication of a number of readable journalistic and academic introductions. Collectively, they have filled a gap in up-to-date and accessible accounts of Taiwan. But Brown also shows how Taiwan can be used to affirm as much as critique unexamined assumptions about a changing world order.

The Taiwan Story begins with a race through Taiwan's history, acknowledging indigenous settlement, the Dutch arrival in the 17th century, their expulsion by the Ming loyalist Koxinga, whose regime was in turn defeated by the Qing empire in 1683, and then, following the empire's halting efforts to govern Taiwan, its cession to Japan as a colonial territory in 1895. In 1945, Taiwan was transferred to the Republic of China (ROC) under the Chinese Nationalists of Chiang Kai-shek – the first attempt to unify Taiwan with a modern Chinese state – which led to the 1947 anti-Chinese Nationalist uprising known as the February 28 incident, or simply "228", and the killing of as many as 30,000 Taiwanese in its suppression. The Nationalists then relocated the ROC government to Taiwan, fleeing the advancing Communists in 1949. They brought an authoritarian developmentalist state with its own Leninist system, until Taiwanese democracy was realised in the late 1980s after decades of violence and struggle that began under Japan in the early 20th century.

That Brown offers this narrative of Taiwan's history is testament to the strength of its affirmation in Taiwan itself. This truly Taiwanese history – different to that propagated by the Chinese Nationalists and certainly by Beijing – moved from activism and academia in the authoritarian era into mainstream Taiwanese public discourse in the 1990s after an intense public debate, especially on education curriculum and policy.

Yet in his summary of the Japanese colonial period Brown includes one line that really stings when he says that Taiwanese people "were either bilingual in Chinese or Japanese, or that Japanese was their first language". Taiwanese were bilingual in Tâi-gí, the Taiwanese language, and Japanese, and this casual conflation elides one of the first acts of the arriving Nationalists in 1945: enforcing the use of Mandarin Chinese. Many older Taiwanese people today still bristle with rage and hurt at a school system in the 1960s and '70s that punished and humiliated them for speaking Taiwanese in class instead of Chinese, just one legacy of the state efforts to remake the Taiwanese as Republican Chinese. Equating Chinese and Taiwanese reflects Brown's struggle throughout the book to fully apprehend Taiwan's distinct modern identity.

The Taiwan Story moves from presenting a historical overview to colourful reportage and analysis of Taiwan's democratic politics and a vigorous account of Taiwan's economic development, concentrating on the story of the semiconductor industry. In semiconductors, Taiwan is the global colossus and China the minnow.

Then Brown pivots to China and the United States. The complex history of Beijing's and Washington's positions on Taiwan have left Taiwan outside the international system, as a state that is not recognised as a state.

For a book on Taiwan to be useful as well as meaningful, it must account for Taiwan's place in US–China relations and the international system. But the great powers exert a gravitational pull on discourse about Taiwan that must be resisted. To fail to do so allows assumptions about Taiwan's identity and its place in the world to seep through until yet again the Taiwanese revert to their metonymic status and are removed from the centre of their own story.

Brown is unable to resist the assumption that Taiwan's exclusion from the international system is a condition for peace between the US and China, which normalises and legitimises Beijing's military threats against the Taiwanese. In its conclusion, *The Taiwan Story* proffers lurid speculative fiction on a future scenario of war, in which, under a bombastic president, the US horrifies the world by recognising Taiwan as a state, and Beijing apparently has no choice but to invade Taiwan and start a war with America. But Beijing always has choices.

Concomitantly, in an imagined alternative of dialogue and peace, Brown assumes there is a quintessential "Chinese" identity that is politically legitimate and emotionally salient enough that it can overcome Taiwan's unique history and identity and allow Beijing to peacefully exercise authority over the Taiwanese in the absence of democratic legitimacy. This conviction hovers on the margins of *The Taiwan Story*, from its opening discussion of Taiwan's identity to its evasive conclusion that, in time, an evolution of identities will bridge the gap between the two sides on China's terms. This idea was tested in 1945, when Taiwan was unified with the Republic of China, and failed utterly in the 1947 uprising.

For an Australian reader, *The Taiwan Story* might fill in much detail about Taiwan's history and politics, yet it might also only affirm assumptions that Taiwan is a choice between the US and China. There is more to do to hear the stories of the Taiwanese people. Australia's choices with Taiwan must start with recognition that, for over a century, its people have been pursuing democracy and sovereignty in parallel to our own national journey.

Mark Harrison

Correspondence

"System update" by Johanna Weaver & Zoe Jay Hawkins

Olivia Shen

Reading "System Update" (Australian Foreign Affairs 24), I was reminded of a conversation with two Canberra policymakers in 2023 who summed up Australia's AI policy as "fast following the United States". It was a disquieting statement then – surely we should aim higher than just fast following? – and is even more so today.

As Johanna Weaver and Zoe Jay Hawkins outline in their essay, the second Trump administration is determined to achieve global AI supremacy. It is so set on winning the AI race against China that any perceived threats to American innovation are in the firing line, whether they are democratic institutions, longstanding trade ties or regulations that curb the power of tech companies.

Australia finds itself in a bind. While many countries would prefer not to choose between Chinese and American technologies, Australia has already chosen. Through an accumulation of policy decisions that are unlikely to be overturned – such as banning the Chinese tech manufacturer Huawei from the national 5G network or AUKUS Pillar 2 – Australia has deeply embedded itself in the US technology ecosystem. When Treasurer Jim Chalmers calls AI "an absolute game changer" for Australia's flatlining productivity, he is talking about AI products that have US fingerprints all over them, from integrated circuits and cutting-edge algorithms to the cloud platforms they run on.

As Weaver and Hawkins point out, Australia must now deal with a US administration that is backing its tech companies in an unprecedented way against friends and foes alike. We have seen, for example, the US hold trade talks with Canada to ransom unless Ottawa scrapped its digital services tax targeting US firms.

Nonetheless, the White House *is* interested in global AI norms. America's AI Action Plan, which President Trump unveiled in July, commits to exporting AI technologies and advocating for global AI governance approaches that "promote innovation, reflect American values, and counter authoritarian influence". The devil is in the detail of how these commitments are operationalised. Behind the diplomatic language, the US has significant leverage over countries that want access to its prized technologies. The worry is that the US will use this leverage to promote pro-business, "America First" policies rather than inclusive, democratic AI.

Weaver and Hawkins recognise that Australia has a degree of tech dependence on the US, but they are ambitious for Australia to do more than simply follow. They propose that Australia should lead an "Interoperable Tech Regulation Initiative" (ITRI), whereby countries unite around shared expectations for the technologies they allow into their markets and marshal their collective bargaining power to go toe-to-toe with the tech giants.

The proposal is a noble one that aims to build solidarity among countries that want to reap the benefits of AI but do not want to end up as roadkill in the AI race. However, a common regulatory framework can only go so far. If ITRI countries lack the sovereign capabilities to build their own technologies and export competitively into each other's markets, China and the US can pick them off one by one through bilateral deals or economic coercion. This is especially true in the case of AI, which requires deep pockets to develop and deploy.

Furthermore, those who command a technology tend to be the ones who set the rules and standards for it. Multilateral instruments have their limitations in a market dominated by a handful of rivalrous players.

Fortunately, many of the "middle-ground nations" mentioned in "System Update" are now making serious investments in sovereign AI. The UK has built a $450-million supercomputer called Isambard-AI to advance British AI research and discovery. India has tapped one of its startups, Sarvam, to build a large language model optimised for India's twenty-two official languages. Closer to home, Japan is investing $1 billion in its domestic chipmaker, Rapidus, while South Korea's new administration has announced a $115-billion plan to develop foundation models trained on Korean data.

In an increasingly contested world, countries recognise that they cannot rely solely on imported technology stacks. Instead, they are turning to homegrown AI tools and infrastructure more suited to their local context and priorities. These efforts might not catapult India or Korea to the lead in AI, or decouple them entirely from Chinese and American products. But they help to diversify supply chains and foster domestic industry and talent.

Australia could be more ambitious in this regard. Our national spending on R&D has been in decline for thirteen years. It currently stands at 1.66 per cent of gross domestic product, well below the 2.7 per cent average across OECD countries. Successive federal governments have been reluctant to make bold investments in public computing and data infrastructure. Even the Future Made in Australia agenda has made few commitments to AI compared to other areas, such as critical minerals and quantum computing, despite having identified AI as a priority. An example of AI infrastructure that could be a strategic asset for Australia is local data centres, which could service not only Australia's growing compute needs but also those of regional neighbours that lack the land, energy or water to host them.

If "System Update" is a call to action for Australia to steer our shared technology future, it should surely also be a call to innovate and create more of the technologies ourselves. Middle-ground nations want more than tech governance; they want tech. Let's lean in on both.

Olivia Shen is the director of the Strategic Technologies Program with the United States Studies Centre at the University of Sydney.

Marina Yue Zhang

In "System Update", Johanna Weaver and Zoe Jay Hawkins argue that technology – particularly AI, digital infrastructure and digital currency – has become both the terrain and the weapon of great-power competition. Under the second Trump administration, they warn, the United States cannot be relied on as a stable steward of the liberal order.

Their core claim is compelling: technology is no longer merely an economic enabler; it now underwrites power, sovereignty and state legitimacy. I broadly agree. The age of techno-geopolitics demands a recalibrated Australian strategy. The authors' proposal for an "Interoperable Tech Regulation Initiative" (ITRI) is timely, as is their call to engage beyond the club of "like-minded democracies". But to turn principle into practice, Australia's aspirations must be grounded in the realities of capability and credibility.

Weaver and Hawkins rightly identify the erosion of state–market boundaries in the United States – symbolised by the Trump-era devolution of tech governance to private actors such as Elon Musk – as symptomatic of deeper institutional decay. But this phenomenon is not unique to America. Globally, governments are outsourcing critical infrastructure to corporate giants. In both China and the US, tech firms are no longer merely partners – they are proxies.

Australia is not immune. Its digital backbone is dominated by large foreign data centres, or "hyperscalers" – among them Amazon Web Services, Microsoft Azure, Apple Pay and Google Maps. This dependency erodes digital sovereignty. Yet Weaver and Hawkins understate the extent of this vulnerability. They also oversimplify Beijing's digital strategy. China's Digital Silk Road – encompassing Huawei's 5G networks, DeepSeek's open-source AI models and the e-CNY central bank digital currency (CBDC) – is more than an authoritarian export. It aims to establish technical norms and digital infrastructure across the Global South.

The authors are right to link AI competition with monetary sovereignty. US dominance in AI (via chips and standards) and in financial plumbing (SWIFT, CHIPS) has long underpinned its global influence. Trump's rejection of a government-backed CBDC in favour of privately issued "stablecoins" – some allegedly tied to his family's business interests – marks yet another erosion of state functions. Beneath that controversy lies a broader shift: market-led, US-dollar-backed stablecoins such as USDT and USDC are emerging partly in response to China's state-led CBDC attempting to de-dollarise global payment systems.

Australia cannot remain a passive adopter of global digital architecture – whether clouds, platforms or payments infrastructure. It must actively shape the frameworks that govern them, championing openness, interoperability and institutional trust. As the authors suggest, Australia's legal design capability and regulatory credibility are strategic assets. But these alone are not sufficient.

I support the authors' call to cultivate an Australian AI ecosystem that is energy-efficient, open-access and geared towards public benefit. But this vision must be grounded in industrial capability. Competing in AI is not only about breakthrough algorithms; it is also about embedding algorithms into the physical economy through logistics, manufacturing, supply chains and critical infrastructure.

Here, China's innovation model offers a lesson. Much of Beijing's technological competitiveness lies not in raw invention but in applied innovation: rapid prototyping, iterative scaling and the integration of AI into its vast industrial base. At the heart of this model are tight-knit industrial clusters, where universities, investors, entrepreneurs and government actors collaborate to co-innovate across sectors. In these ecosystems – which range from smart robotics to AI-optimised supply chains – China has transformed its factory floors into laboratories of technological advancement. This form of "physical AI" is reshaping global production, offering cost-effective and adaptable alternatives to nations seeking digital autonomy – without American price tags.

Australia must invest in sovereign cloud capabilities, open-source tooling, quantum-resilient standards and public-sector AI deployment. Without resilient industrial capacity, Australia cannot credibly lead in the technological order it seeks to shape.

Perhaps the most forward-looking contribution from Weaver and Hawkins is their shift in framing from "like-minded democracies" to "middle-ground countries". This reflects a growing reality: many nations in the Indo-Pacific and beyond prefer not to be conscripted into a binary contest between Washington and Beijing. They seek predictability, transparency and respect for rules-based sovereignty, not ideological alignment.

Australia is well-positioned to lead in this space. If it aims to become a "trusted provider of responsible AI", it must develop and export technologies that are low-cost, bandwidth-sensitive and tailored to regional needs. Such pragmatism would reinforce Australia's credibility across the Indo-Pacific, especially among ASEAN and South Asian partners.

Still, caution is warranted. In an era of weaponised interdependence, countries need to manage risk through diversified, trusted partnerships. Australia's role is not to pick sides between Silicon Valley and Shenzhen but to help design systems that others in the region can trust and use.

That will require more than regulatory elegance. It demands institutional resilience, industrial capability and the quiet discipline of statecraft. ITRI-style alliances can only succeed if they are backed by tangible alternatives: interoperable infrastructure, digital standards and public goods that middle-ground nations are able to adopt. Building sovereign infrastructure, investing in R&D and shaping regional norms are slow, unglamorous tasks. But they are the price of real agency in a fragmented digital order.

As the authors argue, the liberal order may be faltering, but the rules of the new game are still being written. The question is not only what Australia wants to write but how it intends to hold the pen.

Marina Yue Zhang is an associate professor at the Australia-China Relations Institute, University of Technology Sydney.

Johanna Weaver & Zoe Jay Hawkins respond

At the invitation of the editor of Australia Foreign Affairs, we offer this brief response to the correspondence from Olivia Shen and Marina Yue Zhang regarding our essay *System Update: An Australian-led New Deal for Tech.*

Shen is right to urge Australia to aim higher than simply being a "fast follower" on tech regulation, especially if the expectation is that we will follow the United States. The second Trump administration's explicit, erratic and transactional bargaining – paired with its safety-regulation-sceptical, pro-innovation, "anti-woke" approach to AI – do not serve Australia's interests. In recent history, despite exceptions, Australia has enjoyed the relative simplicity of its values and interests usually aligning with those of the United States by default. While it may be jarring to some, the sooner we recognise that this assumption is becoming less reliable, the better positioned we will be to advance Australia's interests in a rapidly changing global order.

Both correspondents support the central call to action in our essay: that Australia should lead a coalition of middle-ground nations to establish the Interoperable Tech Regulation Initiative (ITRI). The ITRI would provide a mechanism for small and medium-sized countries to push back against economic coercion from the United States, China, tech companies or some combination thereof. In a world where democracy is in decline and authoritarian tech – which encodes authoritarian values – is on the rise, it is imperative that states like Australia reassert our right to govern democratically within our own borders.

In different ways, Shen and Zhang both caution against overrelying on regulation and governance to the detriment of investment in Australia and the Australian tech sector. We couldn't agree more. However, we urge readers not to buy into the false dichotomy that regulation and innovation are mutually exclusive. Well-designed regulation builds national capability, drives innovation and boosts productivity. If implemented, long-overdue reforms to Australia's Research and Development Tax Incentive offer an example of regulation that will underpin innovation. Similarly, regulation that reassures users that technology is safe increases public trust and uptake, delivering flow-on productivity gains.

Responding to Shen's and Zhang's calls to prioritise national tech capability, there are several areas in which Australia is well positioned to lead. Cost-effective, energy-efficient AI models that solve real-world problems, cross-border central bank digital currencies and trusted digital government services are three areas we highlighted in the essay. Quantum technologies, robotics and biotech are other areas of Australian competitive advantage.

These tech strengths are not the only basis on which Australia would be well positioned to credibly lead the development of an initiative such as the ITRI. Australia's longstanding leadership during international tech negotiations – at the United Nations, or international standards organisations – combined with our track record of tech regulation domestically, means that when Australia takes the initiative, other counties watch closely.

We agree that diversifying supply chains and boosting sovereign capabilities are important strategies for all countries in managing digital dependency, minimising vulnerability to coercion from either China or the United States and powering innovations at home. Rather than "understating" the vulnerability of weaponised interdependence, our view is informed by the risks it poses and the importance of changing the game.

The reality for most countries – Australia included – is that it is neither feasible nor desirable to become *entirely* self-reliant and cut off from international investment, innovation and capability. We must accept that the United States and China will wield an element of tech stack leverage over third countries for the foreseeable future. And so an assessment purely based on "tech capability" would conclude that such bargaining between the United States and third countries is over before it begins, resulting in countries like Canada being held "to ransom", as Shen says. The purpose of an initiative like the ITRI is to avoid bilateral stand-offs based on digital dependency. Instead, the ITRI could create a diplomatic rebalancing, flip the script and change the strategic calculus for the

United States and China by creating collective opposition to economic coercion and weaponised interdependence.

So while boosting national capability is a vital goal, digital sovereignty is neither a prerequisite nor a meaningful alternative to engaging diplomatically to find strength in numbers to support our interests.

That said, technical capability and regulation are just two of the priorities Australia must navigate. In the Tech Policy Design Institute's latest research spotlight, *Tetris for Australia's Future: Aligning Australia's AI Priorities*, we identify six policy pieces – people and the planet, productivity, trusted institutions and information, regulatory courage, national tech capability, and global governance – that can either align or clash, much like in the game of Tetris. We urge the Albanese government to use its strong second-term mandate to deliver an ambitious and coordinated approach to these interconnected priorities, to lay a strong foundation for Australia's future.

Australia should position itself as a country that builds *and* regulates safe and responsible technology that solves real-world problems. As Zhang rightly notes, most countries in our region and beyond "seek predictability, transparency and respect for rules-based sovereignty, not ideological alignment … Australia's role is not to pick sides between Silicon Valley and Shenzhen but to help design systems that others in the region can trust and use." Positioning Australia to fill this gap – when China and the United States are increasing politicising technology – is a clear competitive advantage for Australia as an exporter of safe and responsible AI for the region. It also makes strategic sense in a world where technological capability increasingly defines the balance of global power.

Ultimately, we agree with both Zhang and Shen that Australia should push the boundaries on diplomatic leadership while simultaneously investing in sovereign tech capabilities. Understanding the different priorities but running both races in parallel is how Australia can actively shape the new world order.

Johanna Weaver is a co-founder of the Tech Policy Design Institute, and formerly Australia's chief cyber negotiator at the United Nations.

Zoe Jay Hawkins is a co-founder of the Tech Policy Design Institute, and a former policy adviser to cabinet ministers, government and Amazon.

The Back Page

FOREIGN POLICY CONCEPTS AND JARGON, EXPLAINED

STRATEGIC INDISPENSABILITY

What is it: "Strategic indispensability" is when a country enhances its power or status by developing technologies or capabilities that no other country has.

Who coined it: Akira Amari (former trade minister, Japan) is believed to have coined the term in a policy paper for Japan's ruling Liberal Democratic Party in December 2020. He urged Japan to develop superconductors and other technologies to make it less dependent on others and to allow it to "grasp the other's chokepoints".

Who likes it: In the European Union, indispensability has been embraced as a solution to the economic vulnerabilities caused by COVID-19, Russia's invasion of Ukraine, and the China–United States rivalry. Georg Riekeles (associate director, European Policy Centre) says the EU should develop clean and emerging technologies as "China builds up its geoeconomic heft… and with an uncertain ally in Trump's America".

In the pipeline: Aside from developing cutting-edge technology, another path to indispensability is to gain a foothold in energy supply chains. In a journal article in July, lead author Rahmat Hajimineh (associate professor, Islamic Azad University) said Türkiye's gas pipelines linking Europe to producers in Russia and the Middle East were "quintessential instruments of geopolitical statecraft, designed to enhance Türkiye's strategic indispensability".

Made in Australia: Naoise McDonagh (senior lecturer, Edith Cowan University) says Australia has a path to indispensability, noting its efforts to process rare earths and break China's dominance of the sector. He wrote in June that Canberra's aim was "to achieve strategic indispensability for the world's leading industrial powers, thereby enhancing Australia's economic security leverage".